James M. Le Count

Holy Hill

Its History, Authentic, Legendary and Prehistoric, In Prose and Poetry

James M. Le Count

Holy Hill
Its History, Authentic, Legendary and Prehistoric, In Prose and Poetry

ISBN/EAN: 9783337155728

Printed in Europe, USA, Canada, Australia, Japan

Cover: Foto ©Thomas Meinert / pixelio.de

More available books at **www.hansebooks.com**

*Its History—Authentic, Legendary and Pre-historic,
in prose and poetry.*

BY J. M. LE COUNT.

ILLUSTRATED.

HARTFORD, WIS.:

J. M. LE COUNT & SON, PRINTERS AND PUBLISHERS.

1891.

To the Reverend N. M. Zimmer, and to his successors, who may hereafter have in their charge the property, and the preservation and safe keeping of the early records of Holy Hill, this book is very respectfully dedicated—

THE AUTHOR.

INTRODUCTION.

In preparing this little volume for its readers the author has labored to give a correct and reliable description, and at the same time, a concise and authentic history of what is locally and popularly known in the eastern portion of Wisconsin as Holy Hill. Though but a small spot within the great universe (only forty acres) yet it has a name and a notoriety of no small importance. It seems to be one of earth's favored precincts; one which the bountiful hand of nature has profusely decorated with rare and charming rural scenery; a retreat for the weary; a spot divinely blest, the hallowed name and romantic beauties of which are destined to endure to the uttermost limits of time.

All that pertains to the hill, geographically, has been gathered by careful research, observation and personal survey, while the distances and altitudes given are from actual measurements taken under the personal supervision of the writer. That portion which relates to its earliest known history, and down to the present time, has been transcribed from well authenticated records, and the whole compiled by one who, for the past forty years, has dwelt approximately within the shadow of the hill.

Whatever is traditional, or merely hear-say, is treated under such especial headings, that none may confound the things that are real, or facts, with those that may admit of contradiction and dispute. Pertaining to such are the "pre-historic" and "traditional" history of the hill. There will also be found an account of the "Hermit," a strange and odd personage, who, for many years, inhabited a rude dwelling in a deep ravine in the hill to the north, and to whose presence there much of the early notoriety of the hill was indebted.

A portion of the work will be devoted to "miracles" or "faith cures," which, are said, to have been wrought from time to time by penitent prayer upon this consecrated ground. Many of them are given as related to the writer by persons of high respectability, and who are apparently sincere in their convictions and firm in their belief. Not a few, but many wonderful cures are vouched for by those who repose implicit faith and confidence in the efficacy of sincere repentance and earnest prayer.

In treating of religion, which is by far the most interesting and attractive attribute of the hill, the writer has endeavored to bestow that deference and respect which are due to all who profess christianity and especially to those who teach the doctrines of Christ.

The illustrations are all from original photographs, taken by a competent artist and transferred totype, by the half toned process, by skillful engravers. They are faithful representations of the scenes they portray.

The author, being an admirer of poetry, and somewhat given to rhyming himself, has introduced several poems of his own composition; not that he claims for them any especial merit, but simply for the reason, that they have the element of originality and may serve to relieve the monotony of lengthy prose readings.

HOLY HILL.

LAPHAM'S RANGE.

IN entering upon this work it may be well to give a brief description of the hill and its surroundings at the outset, that those unacquainted with the locality, as well as the general reader, may form a more correct idea of the formation of the country in which those things of which we are about to speak exist.

Whoever has carefully studied the topography of Wisconsin must have familiarized himself with the very prominent range of hills and lakes located well to the eastern part of the state. This miniature, though well defined mountainous range, has been called by some of the early historians of the state, Lapham's Range, in honor of the late Increase A. Lapham, formerly geologist of the state, and who made a careful survey and study of this extended chain of hills and lakes while Wisconsin was yet a territory.

This range starts out from the most northern extremity of Door county, a peninsula lying between Lake Michigan and Green Bay, and extends in a southwesterly direction for quite two hundred miles, terminating with the four beautiful lakes at Madison, Dane county.

The hills of this continuous range assume such grand proportions in many places as almost to entitle them to the name of mountains, and especially is this true in Washington county. In the towns of Erin, Richfield, Polk and Hartford, the line is more marked, the hills more numerous, are higher and more picturesque than in any other portion of the entire range. In the eastern part of Erin there is a hill, and which forms the central object of this sketch, which for size, grandeur and local notoriety far outranks its fellows in all the lengthy line. It towers high above the surrounding hills and country, forming a conspicuous land-mark that may be seen for a distance of fifteen miles in any direction on a clear day.

Close up to the foot of the hills, and sometimes, as we find, nestling between them, are many beautiful lakes of clear cold water. These are fed by numerous springs that have their source in fountains at the base and on either side of the hills, though by far the greater number and more noted springs are found along the western slope of the range. The lakes are well stocked with many varieties of fish, furnishing abundant sport to the disciples of Isaac Walton, in the season.

The soil among the hills is composed of a yellowish mixture of a heavy clay and loam, though in the valleys it consists of a rich, black alluvial deposit, sediment that has been washed from the hillsides for ages past. The hills are simply huge deposits of clay and lime gravel with occasional strata of fine building sand. Both in the valleys and upon the hills an abundance of large boulders is found, and often some weighing a ton are met with, even on the pinnacles of the highest hills. The hillsides and valleys were originally covered with a heavy growth of hard wood timber, the greater part of which has been cut away to give place for cultivation. The soil is quite productive and many fine farms and thrifty farmers are found among the hills. The scenery that presents itself to the tourist on entering these hills is picturesque and romantic in a high degree; one of ever varying rural beauty that is enchanting and solacing to the lover of quietude, and especially, as here, when combined with Nature's wild and majestic haunts.

In 1881 the author of this book wrote a serial poem entiled "the Hermit of Holy Hill," the first canto of which was published in the West Bend *Times* the same summer. As we shall quote some passages from the poem in this work, we reproduce here that portion descriptive of the foregoing chapter.

LAPHAM'S RANGE.

(FROM THE HERMIT OF HOLY HILL)

Within Wisconsin's broad domain,
  There is a range of hills and lakes,
That from Door county down to Dane,
  Its course we trace which seldom breaks.
A thousand hills along this line
  Unite in one extended row,
Where silv'ry lakes in beauty shine,
  Like mirrors in the vales below.

A thousand rip'ling springs out-gush
  Their waters cold and pure,
And in a hurried race they rush,
  Safe to some lake secure.
A hundred streams on either side
  Start from this lengthy chain,
And wander on by journeys wide;
Though opposite, they seek the tide
  Of ocean's level main.

No lofty range of mountains these,
Like to the Alps or Pyrenees,
Whose snow capped summits to the eye
Appear like icebergs on the sky.
Ours are but hills, yet are we sure
They're mountains still in miniature.
For from a distance they appear
  Like some vast mountain range;
Their summits seem to linger near,
  And with clouds to interchange.

What more of grandeur theirs possess
  In height or vast extent,
Is equaled here by loveliness,
  With Nature's beauties blent.
Here rare and fragrant flowers blush,
  Shedding their sweet perfume,
While fruited vine and hawthorn bush,
  The landscape doth illume.

The whole vaste range one garden lies,
  Where gorgeous scenes expand,
And seems to be earth's paradise,
  By Heavenly wisdom planned:
A paradise where those who roam,
  Would dwell while life is given,
And only quit this rural home
  For an exchange with Heaven.

DESCRIPTION OF THE HILL.

Holy Hill is situated, geographically, in latitude forty-three degrees and eighteen minutes north, and in longitude, eleven degrees and thirteen minutes west from Washington. The hill embraces forty acres of land according to government survey; being described in the survey book of Wisconsin, as the southwest quarter of the northeast quarter of section fourteen, in township No. nine north, (Erin) and in Range No. eighteen east of the principal meridian.

The entire forty acre tract is one grand assemblage of lofty hills and peaks, piled together fantastically and promiscuously as to size and height. They are huddled closely together and in many instances only separated by narrow and deep ravines. The surface of the whole tract is so rough and uneven that no one acre entire could be cultivated with any degree of profit. The greatest altitude attained by any one of the group of hills is that known as Holy Hill, though that name is commonly applied to the whole forty acres. This grand peak rises to a height of two

DISTANT VIEW OF HOLY HILL, LOOKING WEST.

hundred and eighty-nine feet above its base; eight hundred and twenty-seven feet above the surface level of lake Michigan and fourteen hundred and nine feet above the level of the sea. It is the highest point of land in eastern Wisconsin and the second highest in the state; one peak of the Blue Mounds in Dane county being seventeen hundred and twenty-nine feet above the sea level.

Here the range of hills extends through the town of Erin on a line nearly north and south, its deviation being a little to the east of north after leaving the south township line. It is continuous and unbroken throughout its whole extent; the different elevations showing separate outlines standing like so many sugar loaves ranged along the line. From whichever direction one approaches the hills, one, tall and conical in shape, towers high above all others, and challenges his attention and admiration, no less by its lofty height than by the beauty and symmetry of its outline. Its sides are heavily wooded to near its very crest, whereon there is now standing a large brick church, which, when viewed from a distance, has the appearance as if hung in the sky. It rises gracefully from the very apex and towers high above the hills and surrounding country; a guide for the tourist and a beacon for the weary pilgrim who seeks with faith and piety its sacred threshold.

Holy Hill is located on the southeast quarter of the forty acres, its summit being equi-distant from the east and south line and about twenty-five rods distant from either point. The eastern and southern slopes are the most abrupt and precipitous; that to the east rising at an angle of less than thirty degrees from a perpendicular. Were it not for the thick undergrowth of timber, which covers the side of the hill, affording a good hand and foothold at every step, it would be next to impossible for any human being to ascend the hill from that point of compass. The most easy route by which to reach the summit of the hill is by the winding roadway leading from the gate at the northeast corner of the hill. To reach the summit by this route one must climb to a height of two hundred and six feet from the gateway, and tread a crooked pathway eighteen hundred and sixty-three feet in length, making an average rise of about one foot in nine.

The whole tract is covered with a dense growth of natural forest, which has been carefully and sacredly preserved in all its orginal beauty. Protected by parochial injunction, it is deemed an act of sacrilege for one to cut or remove a single tree or shrub from the sacred enclosure, without having first obtained permission. From half way down, to the base of the hill, and through the deep ravines, are seen many trees of larger growth, such as white and red oak, elm, basswood, maple and butternut. Farther up, the hillsides are thickly covered with a forest of second growth timber, consisting of oak, wild cherry, poplar, ash, hickory, and an occasional white birch. Underneath the larger growth the whole surface is thickly covered with a shrubbery of sumach, hazel, osier, crab-apple, wild plum, and hawthorn; among which are profusely mingled blackberry, raspberry and gooseberry bushes; while here and there, over all, the clinging wild grape, ivy, woodbine and bitter-sweet vines grow rank and luxuriant. The very hill-

top, owing to its exposed condition, being subject to
frequent terrific storms of wind, is but a barren and
gravelly waste, destitute of trees and with but
scanty vegetation.

On reaching the summit of the hill, for the first
time, one experiences a feeling of wonderment and
awe on beholding the magnificent scene spread out
far below and around him. On every side, stretching
away to the horizon, as far as the vision can reach,
he views from its centre a most beautiful panorama
which completely encircles him. Due north and four
miles away, is seen Pulford's Peak and Pike Lake
nestling close to its western base; directly on the
same line, and eight miles distant, is seen the large
Catholic church at St. Lawrence; a little to the left,
Hartford, with its many tall church spires, shows
plainly, and is exactly five and a half miles distant
on a straight line. A little east of north is seen the
large and little Cedar lakes. Looking east, St.
Augustine's church, though a mile and a half away,
appears quite close at hand; while beyond, a glimmer
of Frieze's lake is caught in the distance. To the
south is the valley of the east branch of the Oconomowoc river, and Loew's lake is plainly seen, as are
also, many of the beautiful lakes of Waukesha county;
while farther to the west, and twenty miles away,
Prospect Hill, near Delafield, looms up against the
sky. To the west the broad valley of Rock River is
plainly outlined,, beyond which the rolling prairies
of Dodge county appear. Over this broad expanse,
of fifteen miles radius, hundreds of farm buildings and
well cultivated farms dot and decorate the landscape
like so many fruitful gardens. High hills and fertile

valleys intervening, forests and groves, lakes and rivers, cities and villages all within the scope of instantaneous vision! By the aid of a good field glass, with a clear atmosphere, many objects of interest are clearly discernible; among which, to the southeast, is the spire of the Catholic cathedral and a number of the higher structures of Milwaukee, and still farther to the south, the smoke from the rolling mills at Bay View; west, the court house at Juneau, Dodge county and to the northwest the state's prison at Waupun.

HOLY HILL.

(FROM THE HERMIT OF HOLY HILL)

In Erin's township to the east,
　There is a hill that wears the crown—
The monarch of the range, at least
　In height, in grandeur and renown.
It towers above all others there;
　Its rugged sides loom high and hoar;
They mount to meet and mingle where
Its lofty summit, bleak and bare,
　Looks down from whence the eagles soar.

Each crag and hill top doth proclaim—
　"This place, how sacred, and divine!
Created thus, and will remain
　Through all the years of coming time."
Around its base the forest wild,
　Stands just as nature placed it there,
By human hands still undefiled—
　'Twere sacrilege, and none should dare
　Despoil its sacred beauties rare.

The sun's first beams still light its crest,
　As on creation's natal day;
And when departing in the west,
　Still sheds o'er it its latest ray.
The hills, the forest, glade and glen,
　All here intact, untouched by time;

Unchanged the scene, the same as when,
 That bold explorer, Joliet,*
And Holy Father, James Marquette,
 First viewed these lofty peaks sublime.

Beyond dispute, the records show,
These men—two hundred years ago—
In sixteen hundred seventy-two,
Here sought to find a passage through
These wilds, and by it thought to gain
The Mississippi's mystic main,
 And solve its unknown hidden might.
They thought to gain Rock river's side,
Thence by its current safely glide.
 To where their waters did unite.

But here they halted, and retraced
 Their steps, as from this summit high,
They viewed the far off western waste,
 And saw no river wandering nigh.
Yet ere they left, from where they gazed,
 Here on the summit's topmost sod,
A rude and ponderous cross they raised
 And offered prayers and praise to God.
And long it stood there, queer and quaint,
 Through fear no savage dared destroy—
The cross was raised to Mary Saint—
 The hill they chris'ened *Butte des Bois.*

---

*Reference to this passage is made in the "traditional history" of this work.

A winding pathway from the north,
  Leads to the summit of this hill,
Which having gained, and looking forth,
  You feel an instant inward thrill—
A sense of wonder, mixed with awe,
As doubting what your vision saw—
As though your wayward footsteps trod
A trifle nearer to your God.
You see a landscape stretching wide,
Around, below, on every side,
Far as the human eye can wander,
It sights a scene of gorgeous grandeur.

Here charming lakes in bright array,
  Lend an enchantment to the view,
And rivers wandering far away,
  Their onward, restless course pursue.
Each home and hamlet dots the land,
  Like stars upon the heaven's expanse,
While fruitful fields on every hand,
  The beauties of the scene enhance.

Here hill-tops rear their lofty heads,
  And stand like sentries o'er the scene,
To guard the haunts where beauty spreads
  Her couch in sylvan groves serene.
While o'er this picture, grand and wide,
  From vale below to summits' sod;
In objects seen on either side,
  Is recognized the hand of God.

EARLY SETTLEMENT.

THIS chapter, though digressing somewhat from the main subject, is introduced here as showing how, when and by whom, the immediate country surrounding Holy Hill was first settled; matters which had their weight in fashioning the subsequent features of the work before us.

One very peculiar and distinctive feature in regard to the early settlement of Wisconsin, was the large number of colonies that were settled in each instance exclusively by a people of the same nationality. In various districts they came in one body, into each, from the same country and from the same locality in the fatherland. No other state in the union has so many different nationalities living in communities where the inhabitants of each are so distinctively homogeneous as Wisconsin. It was so from the first, and the lapse of fifty years has not materially altered its original condition.

One very noteworthy national group was formed

as early as 1842 in and around Holy Hill. Township nine in Washington county was settled, with a few rare exceptions, exclusively by the Irish, and naturally they named the town Erin. This large and purely Irish settlement was not however confined to the town of Erin alone, but included nearly the entire two southern tiers of sections in Richfield, and also the north and west portions of the town of Merton in Waukesha county.

Michael Lynch has the distinction of being the first settler in Erin. He made the first entry of land in Erin on the 27th day of November, 1841, being forty acres in section thirty-five, and situated just three miles directly south from Holy Hill. This entry was followed by that of Eleazer Rowley, who entered forty acres in section twenty-five, three miles southeast of the hill on the same day, two hours later.

During the succeeding two years nearly every available acre in the township had been entered. The first town meeting was held at the house of Patrick Toland on section twenty-nine, April 6, 1846, and at which seventy-four votes were cast. The officers elected were William Dwire, Chairman; Thomas Carroll, and John Lynch, Supervisors, Thomas Fitzgerald, Clerk; John Kenny, Treasurer; Michael Healey and William Foley, Assessors; Thomas Carroll and William Paulding, Justices of the Peace; Thomas Burke, Timothy McNamara and James Lynch, School Commissioners and William Sullivan, Collector.

The early settlers of Erin were, to a unit, steadfast adherents of the Roman Catholic Church. The first mass ever said in the town was by the Rev.

Father Kundig, in the log house of Barney McConville on section twenty-two, in September 1844. Rev. Kundig made his advent into Erin on foot, coming up from Prairieville (now Waukesha) by the way of Merton and Monches. Soon after, the citizens assisted in building a log church at Monches where the early settlers of Erin worshipped for a number of years.

They have now two Catholic churches in the town. One, St. Patrick's, located in the centre of section nine, one and a half miles south of the north township line. It is a wooden structure, quite commodious and substantially built. It stands on the east of the main highway on a gentle rise of ground and from its commanding position can be seen for miles around. Just west from the church, and across the highway, is the "silent city," large and cleanly kept, where, on polished white marble are recorded the names of a majority of Erin's pioneers who, "have laid them down in their last sleep." Two miles to the southeast of St. Patrick's, stands the other church, St. Mary's Help on Holy Hill, and of which further mention will be made.

The majority of the early settlers of Erin came in from nearly the same locality in Ireland; coming principally from Cary, Cork and adjoining counties. They were apparently descendants from a small number of original families, as in many instances the relationship of one extended through a long line of his fellow compatriots. Most of the older ones spoke the Irish or Celtic language, and when in conversation among themselves they spoke that in preference to any other.

In many respects Erin is completely isolated from the outside business world. It is exclusively a farming town, having no factory of any kind, no village, no telegraph or telephone and no railroad. It has only one store, and near it the postoffice is kept. The mail is brought to this office twice a week from Hartford.

The township, being strictly an agricultural one, seems to have reached its limit as to population, and for years it has shown no material increase. Its population was 1266 in 1870; 1273 in 1880 and 1301 in 1890.

Coming from the same country and locality, bound together by the ties of wedlock or consanguinity, and worshippers at the same altar, it is no wonder that they should have been as one on political questions, as they assuredly were. No town in this state was ever so totally democratic as Erin. For years it was the banner democratic town of Washington county, and for twelve years subsequent to its first organization no non-democratic vote was ever cast at its polls. But in 1860 its unique record was broken by Abraham Lincoln, who received in the town of Erin, one vote for president. Since that date, at times as high as fifty votes have been cast in the town for the opposite party.

It does not appear that the old settlers of Erin were actuated by that spirit of progress and improvement so characteristic of their sons to-day. But this was no doubt owing to the difficulties and hardships incident to pioneer life; or else they were not possessed of the means necessary to carry out their ideas in this direction. Be that as it may, it was a noticeable fact that very few fine residences and commodious farm buildings were met with in Erin until within the past few years. The older people seemed happy and contended, and rather preferred to remain in their humble log cabins that had served them for a home since their advent into the wilderness, than to dwell in homes of luxury unpaid for. There are many instances extant in Erin to-day, where the log cabin of nearly fifty years existence still serves as a home for its original owner.

An instance of this kind is shown in the accompanying engraving of the home of Mr. Christopher McGuire. The photograph, after which the engraving was made, was taken in May of the present year. Although Mr. McGuire entered his land from government in 1844, he has lived continually on it ever since. His farm, which consists of seventy-eight acres, adjoins Holy Hill on the north, and his log dwelling, seen at the left hand of the picture, is just eighty rods due north of the northwest corner of the hill property. His log barn and stable, at the right, are well dilapidated. A log granary is seen mid-way between the house and barn, while the two small buildings, half dug-outs in the hill, are a milk house at the left, and the hen house at the right. The high hill in the background is of the range of hills, while in the foreground is shown a natural pond or lake. In the lower right hand corner of the cut, is seen a small portion of the highway leading to Holy Hill.

Those who have previously visited the hill, going by the way of Hartford, will recognize the place by the picture at the first glance; while those, who may hereafter visit it for the first time may know, when

HOME OF CHRISTOPHER McGUIRE.

they reach this spot, that they are near their journey's end, and forty rods farther to the east the hill, which for the last mile has been hidden from view by intervening hills, will be seen upon the right standing in all its stately grandeur and rural beauty close at hand.

Twenty rods farther to the east brings you to the gateway of the private road which leads directly south to the hill, only eighty rods distant from the entrance to the sacred enclosure. In former years this private road was the property of Mr. Matthias Werner, who owned the land adjoining on the east. Through his generosity the public was for years permitted to pass over it free, to and from the church grounds, but as it was private property no road work was bestowed upon it and it was generally in poor condition for travel. But in the fall of 1890, through the instrumentality of Rev. N. M. Zimmer of Hartford, who was the custodian of the church property at the hill, a strip of land twenty-five feet wide and eighty rods long, leading from the highway to the hill, was bought from Mr. Werner for one hundred dollars. This roadway has since been graded and put in fine condition, making it one of the best quarter mile drives between Hartford and the hill.

The point where the bye-road diverges from the main highway affords as fine a view of the hill as can be had anywhere. From here nearly the whole of the north, and a portion of the east side of the hill, stand out plainly before you, and the church on the summit is distinctly outlined against the sky. From here can be seen station one, near the gateway, and from where the steep and winding pathway leading to the church on the extreme hill-top begins.

At this point it was the custom, in an early day, for visitors to the hill to halt and leave their horses and carriages in charge of Roman Goetz, who lived on the north side of the high-way; or with his son-in-law, Mr. Matthias Werner, who lived a few rods farther to the east. Both of these men were very obliging and hospitable to those who visited the

WERNER'S HOTEL, NEAR HOLY HILL.

hill, and especially to strangers. Mr. Goetz was the custodian of the church property, and from him the key to the old chapel, that stood where the new church now stands, could be obtained. In the early times Mr. Werner kept a sort of a hotel, where tourists and pilgrims to the hill were entertained. Feed for horses, good lodging and a substantial meal could always be obtained, and at a low price at Werner's hotel in an early day. Besides providing for the wants of the inner man, Mr. Werner did all in his power to make his guests happy while under his hospitable roof.

Viewed from this point, at any season of the year, the hill presents a scene that is attractive and pleasing to the eye; but to see it in all its majesty and splendor, one must visit this spot about the latter part of September or when the early frosts, alternated with the scorching rays of an autumn's sun, has transformed the foliage into colors gay and manifold. It is at this season of the year that the hill appears at its best; looking like a beautiful picture spread upon an immense canvas, in bright and charming colors of every hue and shade.

The magnificent coloring of the foliage by an American autumn is a sight not met with in any other country in the world, and many people yearly cross the sea merely to gaze upon its beauties. But even here, not every locality is favored with the imposing sight. All necessary conditions must be present to produce the grand effect. These conditions require a latitude between forty and forty-five degrees north; a forest where many varieties of trees, shrubs and creeping vines grow dense, and the different kinds are well distributed. Added to these, the forest should be located upon a hill-side, so that the many colors and shadings are distinctly brought to view. Under such conditions only, do you find in all its entirety, the really magnificent American autumn scene.

THE AUTUMN SCENE.

(FROM THE HERMIT OF HOLY HILL.)

There's but one time in all the year,
  To view aright this wond'rous pile—
Yet be alone, have no one near,
  For Nature's beauties only smile
And yield their rarest charms profound
To him who hears no human sound.

Go see this hill in beauty fringed,
When autumn's frost has touched and tinged
  Its foliage with a thousand hues,
And spread them like a robe of state
In gorgeous garb, elaborate,
  Beyond conceptions of the muse,
Or painter's power to imitate.

From where the hill-top frets the sky,
  Thence downward to the lowland glade,
'Tis mantled o'er in richest dye,
  Of every color, hue and shade.
Around its summit, bare and brown,
A belt of osiers forms a crown
Of green, that early frost defies,
And clings to life when verdure dies.

While here and there along this zone,
  The sumac waves its gaudy plume
And stamps it with a richer tone—
  In brighest colors of maroon.
Then blending with, and just below,
The deeper lines of yellow show
Where poplars stand in graceful pride,
With wild grape clinging to the side,
In verdure green, which droops and sways;
Each passing breeze its fruit displays
And shows the ripeness and the luster
Of many a pendant purple cluster.

Here lindens wave their orange leaves,
  Which to the scene rich tributes yield;
Arrayed like shocks of golden sheaves
  Upon some late reaped harvest field.
To make this painting all complete,
On every hand the eye doth greet
The coral-berried bitter-sweet.

The ivy, wild, whose crimson shade,
  Wrought by alternate frost and heat,
Droops gay from many a trunk decayed—
Like master-strokes by artists made;
  The final touch, that makes complete,
And gives the picture grace and tone
When viewed in solitude, alone.

Here maples wide their branches spread,
  And casts a lustre which imbues
The whole with splendor, where they shed
  Their colors of a thousand hues.

The hazel blends its dusky brown
From base below to summit crown;
  While down within the dark ravine,
  The giant oak in mantle green
  Adds grandeur to the autumn scene.

Go stand below and cast your eye
  Far upward on this colored dome;
Behold this picture on the sky!
  No matter where your footsteps roam,
You ne'er will meet a scene like this—
Replete with nature's loveliness;
On earth a Heavenly Paradise.

A CHANGE OF NATIONALITY.

WE come now to a most singular page in the history of the early settlement of the town of Erin; a transformation from an Irish to a German population and especially in the neighborhood of Holy Hill. With one single exception there has been an absolute change in this direction of five entire sections in the northeast part of the town, and a partial change in at least five others. And this change is still progressing, and at a rate that bids fair at no distant day to depopulate the Irish of fully one half their original settlement.

It is difficult to account for this radical transmutation upon any theory other than the proximity of the city of Milwaukee, with its large German population. Many of these, daily laborers and possessed of some means, were ever ready and on the lookout for a chance to change their position as wage workers for the more quiet and peaceful pursuits of farm life. Here, and close at hand, the golden opportunity for such a change presented itself. For the farms in the "hills," which were quite rough and without many improvements, could be bought of the original owners much cheaper than farms in more favorable localities. While on the other hand the Irish that settled among the hills in an early day were comparatively poor, and their experience with pioneer life for ten or fifteen years had only brought them a mere living at the expense of many privations and much hard labor; and they, as a class, generally preferring the city to country life, were quite willing to sell, the first opportunity that offered, and especially when they could do so at a profit. Be this as it may the change was inaugurated as early as 1854, and has been slowly increasing to the present time.

However, the transfers made by the Irish to the Germans, thus far, only include the more rough and uneven portion of the town, while all the very best farming land is still in possession of the original owners or their direct descendants, and in all probability will so remain for many years to come. Within the last fifteen years there has been a marked improvements among the Irish farmers of Erin, and the thrift is noticeable on every hand, from the good cultivation of their farms, and excellent improvements in fencing, roads and the many fine farm buildings that are now being built every year.

Though the Germans have, as yet, become the possessors of only the poorer class of farming lands; yet by their thrift and industry, so characteristic of that class of people, they have already converted the rough and seemingly barren waste into very productive farms. Those who were acquainted with the thriftless condition of things among the "hills," even fifteen years ago, if they pass through them to-day, will be greatly surprised with the many substantial improvements which have been wrought in that short space of time.

As previously stated in this work there were a few exceptional cases, where the early settlers of Erin were people of nationalities other than Irish. These exceptions were limited to about six or seven Norwegian families who took up land from government on the extreme western edge of the town. Also Jacob Loew, a German, who entered nearly all the land in section twenty-five and one quarter of section twenty-six. John Krauter, also a German, occupied forty acres in the southeast corner of section twenty-four in a very early day, though he may have purchased it second hand. These, and possibly one or two others, were the only exceptions to the otherwise exclusively Irish settlement of Erin.

The great change in the population began when Matthias Werner purchased the forty acres just at the foot, and to the northeast of the hill, from Thomas Benningham, in the summer of 1854. Mr. Werner did not occupy or live on the place until two years later. In 1856 he married a daughter of Romanus Goetz, and removed to the farm which he has occupied continually ever since. His father-in-law followed him, making his home with him for a few years. He then bought two acres of land from Christopher McGuire, just opposite the bye-road leading up to the hill. Here Mr. Goetz built him a house in which he lived for many years. Both Mr. Werner and his father-in-law, Mr. Goetz, were Prussians, their homes in the old country being near Koehlen on the upper Rhine near the boundaries of Switzerland.

The style of architecture used in the construction of the home of Roman Goetz is widely different from that used by the early Irish settlers in the construction of their log cabins. To show this contrast, a *fac simile* of his home is given on the opposite page. It is a genuine copy of a Swiss cottage, as used by the peasantry of the country from which he emigrated. It is still standing by the roadside and is in a good state of preservation.

HOME OF ROMAN GOETZ.

TITLE TO THE HILL.

THE forty acre tract comprising Holy Hill, owing to the fact that it was valueless for farming purposes, remained a number of years as government property. Long after all the land in the vicinity had been entered, and as late as 1855, the Rev. Francis Paulhuber entered the land; and as the circumstances which led him to make the entry are somewhat interesting, and the subsequent history of the hill has so wonderfully verified a prophecy, made by him before he became the actual possessor of the property, it is deemed worthy of particular mention here.

At the date above mentioned, Father Paulhuber was the local priest of the neighborhood, and had charge of three parishes; St. Boniface, at Goldenthal, in the town of Germantown; St. Hubert's, on section twenty-two in the town of Richfield and St. Augustine's in Richfield, on the range line and only a little over a mile to the east of Holy Hill. While officiating at the latter church he made his home with Joseph Kohler, who lived a half mile south of St. Augustine's church and a mile and a quarter directly east of the hill.

Father Paulhuber was a native of Salsburg, Austria, and was born and educated to the priesthood in that country. It was while stopping at Mr. Kohler's in the fall of 1854, and while viewing the Hill, which shows up grandly from this point that he made the wonderfully true prophecy before mentioned. Said he, pointing to the west. "That beautiful hill yonder, reminds me very forcibly of a hill near our home in my native country. I feel very sure and the day is not far distant, when that hill will become one of the most noted places in all this land; when it shall be consecrated and made holy; a place of worship and a pilgrimage where tens of thousands shall yearly come to do homage to the Virgin Mary and her Son. Only lately have I learned that the hill is still owned by the government, and it is my intention to secure it without delay, and then permanently establish the title by deed to this Arch-Diocese of the Roman Catholic church." This declaration was made in the presence of a number of his parishioners, a few of whom are still living.

That Father Paulhuber carried out the first part of his intention as stated is quite certain, for the records show that he entered the land from government, May 1st, 1855, by duplicate No. 38,710. It is also reasonably sure that the entire promise was fulfilled on his part, though no deed appears on the records from him to the bishop of the Arch-Diocese. It is stated, however, and on good authority, that he did execute a deed before the late John M. Gans, who resided in the neighborhood, and who was then a Notary Public. It is thought that Rev. Paulhuber must have left the deed with Mr. Gans, with instructions to have it placed on record, and then send it to the grantee named in the deed. But this important matter was undoubtedly overlooked and forgotten, as the people in those early days were not so particular to record papers as most all are at the present time. Soon after Father Paulhuber returned to his home in the old country and died there. Mr. Gans has since died, and in all probability there is no witness to the transaction living at the present time, though there are some still living who have a vivid recollection that the transfer of the Hill property was made by Father Paulhuber as above stated.

The negligence in not placing Paulhuber's deed on record caused a serious complication in the title of the land to arise, which was not perfected for years, nor then without great trouble and some expense. Had his deed been recorded, showing it to be church property, it would have escaped assessment and taxation; but being recorded in Paulhuber's name it was considered private property and as such was assessed and taxed. It next appears, by the records, that the land was sold for taxes, and was bought by one Martin L. Cutler. This Cutler was a sort of a "money shark," and ever on the alert to take advantage of the poor settlers who, in the early days were unable to pay their taxes when due. This

many of the pioneers, not only of Erin but of every
town in the county, can testify to, to their sorrow
to-day.

Cutler's deed from Washington county bore date
of August 13, 1856, and was recorded seven days
later. There was evidently a mistake in the description of the land in this deed, as it followed too soon
after Paulhuber's deed from government; much
sooner than the law prescribes for deeding lands for ·
taxes. As such are the facts, it follows that some
other land was sold for taxes, and by an error the
description of the hill property was inserted in
Cutler's deed. However he continued to hold it and
pay the taxes assessed against it for twelve years
following the date of his deed.

The next recorded conveyance to the Holy Hill
property was a quit-claim deed given by Martin L.
Cutler and wife to Washington county, under date
of March 9th, 1868. Just what inducement led
Mr. Cutler to make this sale is not known to the
writer. Certainly, it was not the price he received
for it, as the consideration named in the deed was
only about nine dollars, a sum hardly sufficient to
reimburse him for his first outlay and the interest on
that for twelve years.

It seems that this deed from Cutler and wife to
Washington county was the iniatory step taken by
the authorities of the Catholic Church to perfect the
title to the property, and to restore it to the church
as was the original intent of Father Paulhuber. For
following close upon the date is found a recorded
quit-claim deed from Washington county to the trustees of St. Mary's Chapel in the town of Erin. This

deed is dated November 5th, 1868, and was placed on record the same day. The consideration named in this deed is ten dollars.

Here the title to the hill property rested for nearly eight years more, and, as will be seen later on, many improvements were added to the place during that interval of time. It was also during those years and the five years immediately preceding, that the hill gained its great notoriety as a shrine of sacred pilgrimage; a resort where those devotionally inclined might worship in solitude alone; a notoriety from which all subsequent years have detracted nothing but, on the contrary, have rather increased its popularity and extended its field of patronage until to-day it has a fame and a renown that have no parallel among the institutions of its kind anywhere upon the western continent.

We come now to the last recorded transfer of the Holy Hill property. This is a quit-claim deed from Romanus Goetz, John Piek and Bertram Schwarz, as trustees of St. Mary's Chapel in the town of Erin, Washington County, Wisconsin, to Rev. John Martin Henni, arch-bishop of the Milwaukee Arch-Diocese of Wisconsin. This deed bears the date of May 26th, 1876, and was recorded June 24th, 1876, in volume thirty-six of deeds, on page seventeen. The consideration named in this deed is just one dollar, being only the nominal fee fixed by law for transfers made by gift or donation.

The last transfer fixes the title to the property securely, and undoubtedly forever, in the name of the Roman Catholic church, and where the Rev. Francis Paulhuber had previously, no doubt, intended it should be nearly forty years ago. Though the title was for many years in the name of Martin L. Cutler by a tax deed, and for a time in the name of Washington county by a quit-claim deed from him, yet the title of Cutler must have always been considered as faulty, for at no time during these years did the members of the Catholic church ever relinquish their possession to it; but from the first they continued to occupy it and build improvements there. This tenure to the land was based upon their knowledge or belief, that Paulhuber, before his departure for his home in the old country, did donate the property to their church by his own free act and deed. Therefore their possession to it has been continuous and has remained undisturbed from the government down to the present time.

HOW TO REACH THE HILL.

A s previously stated, the location of the hill is just five miles distant from Hartford, on an air line, in a southeasterly direction; though the distance one must travel to reach it is a little more than six and a half miles, caused by the road deviating many times from a direct course.

There are three stations on the railroads which are the most convenient for tourists to leave the cars and make their way by carriage conveyance to the hill. Schleisingerville, on the Northern Division of the Chicago, Milwaukee & St. Paul, and also on the Wisconsin Central R. R., is eight miles from the hill by the nearest wagon road. The direction from this station is a little west of south. Richfield on the St. Paul road is distant seven and a half miles by the nearest route. From this station the line of travel is due west. The road from Schleisingerville, and

also that by the way of Richfield, are both beset
with many intervening hills, a few of which are very
steep and lengthy.

It is quite obvious that the route to the hill by
the way of Hartford is by far the most preferable,
when we consider the facts that it is fully a mile
nearer than either of the two last mentioned places,
and that the road is less hilly; in addition to which
Hartford affords good livery accommodations, a
convenience that is wanting in either of the other
places.

To reach the hill from Hartford by the nearest
and most convenient way one should take the State
road south. Before leaving the city limits the hill is
seen directly before you looming up in the southeast. It remains plainly in sight for nearly the whole
journey, though at times it is lost to sight by the
intervening hills. The road south should be continued for two miles, or to the school house on the
town line between Hartford and Erin. Then the
direction is east for one and a half miles, or to the
foot of the range of hills. At this point you are a
little more than half way, and the distance traveled
has been nearly level. Here the direction is again
south for two miles, when the turn is again east, and
three-quarters of a mile farther brings you to the
bye-road leading up to the hill. It makes no difference
from which railroad station one's pilgrimage begins,
all must surely centre at this point.

In the annexed engraving is shown the Temperance
Saloon of Peter McGuire, standing on the southwest
corner of the highway and the bye-road. In the
lower left hand corner of the cut, near the gate, is

shown the down hill and abrupt turn onto the bye-road only eighty rods from the gateway to Holy Hill.

When the photograph was taken, after which the engraving was made, in May of the present year, the sign above the door read "Temperance Saloon and

MC GUIRE'S SALOON AND GROCERY.

Grocery." Since then the proprietor seems to have taken a backward step, as the word "Temperance" has since been erased.

The drive from Hartford to the hill is a very pleasant and romantic one, and requires about one hour's time under favorable circumstances, which include a good team, roads and weather.

For the first half of the journey the road leads through a delightful farming country where thrift and enterprise are noticeable upon either hand. Soon after leaving the school house you cross a beautiful stream, the headwaters of the Ashippun river, and which has its source from numerous springs in the bluffs a mile farther to the east. At the foot of the hills are seen upon either hand many beautiful springs of clear cold sparkling water. Here the tired wayfarer usually halts to rest and slake his thirst at some one of the cool fountains by the wayside, the streams of which are heavily cress laden.

From here to the hill the road is more rough and hilly. Soon you pass the little white church on the right with its tall and graceful spire pointing upward to the blue vault of Heaven, while to the north and rear is spread out God's Acre, as yet but sparsely populated. Then you ascend the long hill and on reaching the top, Holy Hill is seen before you, a little to the left, and two miles away. From here the sight is beautifully grand, and must have caused many a pilgrim's heart to beat for joy when he reached the brow of this hill and beheld the goal of his pilgrimage so near at hand. The tall and symmetrical form of the hill is distinctly outlined against the southern sky; while from its apex, and completely capping it, gracefully rises the church, its light grey color being in marked contrast with the hill's dark green sides. Above all the gilded "cross in the sky," like to that seen by Constantine and his followers, flashes back the bright rays of sunlight, to beckon and guide the weary pilgrim on his way.

As you near the hill the road grows rougher and

more picturesque. At times you go down into fertile
valleys, then mount again some high and rugged hill.
The scene around you is suddenly transformed, and
you find yourself surrounded by a haunt where the
most primitive of human habitations are. The
houses and barns which are built of logs, show age
and decay, and some are tenantless. Old fashioned
rail fences and broken down stone walls line the
roadsides and mark the divisions of separate individual domains. These are half hidden with the
creeping vines of grape, bitter-sweet, honey-suckle
and wild hops, and all are supplemented with a dense
growth of thorn, hazel and sumac, forming a barrier
seemingly strong enough to resist the encroachments
of beasts or even man. The whole country now
presents such a varied contrast to the fine fertile
farms passed by when the journey began that one
enjoys the scene the more, for its wild, rural and
romantic aspect.

ORIGIN OF THE NAME.

With regard to the different names that have been given to the hill in times past, and that by which it is generally known at the present time, this chapter will be entirely devoted. In fact, its name has been changed quite often to suit the times and circumstances which surrounded its history in the days gone by.

It will follow in the traditional part of this work that the first explorers of the west, Joliet and Father Marquette, in 1672, gave it the name of *Butte des Bois*—Hill of the Woods—Though there is nothing very authentic regarding this, yet it is quite certain that the early French so called it, and it was also so written in their old manuscripts, some of which are still extant. However, as to this, we shall introduce more testimony in a subsequent portion of this work.

Coming down to the earliest authentic name given to the hill, we find it recorded in history as LAPHAM'S PEAK. This was in honor of the late Increase A. Lapham, once state geologist, and who made a scientific study and survey of the range of hills, which also bears his name in history, long before Wisconsin was admitted into the Union as a state.

Perhaps the most commonplace, and at the same time really literal name ever given to the hill, was the one applied to it by the first inhabitants who settled in that immediate neighborhood. They gave it no euphonious or high sounding title, but called it simply, the BIG HILL. By that name it was known and called by the first settlers for many years. Though the name is gradually growing into disuse and destined to become obsolete at no distant day, still there are a few of the older inhabitants who, in speaking of the hill, continue to call it by that name, even at the present time.

It will appear in a subsequent chapter, that which treats of the history of the church at the hill, that a cross was raised on its highest elevation. The cross was raised and blest in the summer of 1858 by Rev. J. B. Hasselbauer, who then had charge of several parishes in Richfield, and particularly St. Augustine's in the immediate vicinity. The cross and the hill were dedicated in the name of St. Mary, and from that time, and until quite recently, the hill was called by all members of the Catholic church, ST. MARY'S HILL. In fact, a large majority of the members of that church still continue to call it by that name to-day.

The time when the cross was raised and blest was
some time before any other church improvements
were made. It was four years later when the little
rude log chapel on the hill was built; though the
church era proper, dates from the raising and blessing
of the cross. From that time, and down to the year
of 1881, there was no other name excepting St.
Mary's Hill, applied to the place by the members of
the Catholic church. The name is still retained and
used by the older members, and in all probability will
be for many years to come.

In the month of June, 1862, four years after the
cross had been erected, there appeared in the vicinity
a very strange personage; a man of mature years,
peculiar in his traits and odd in his dress and manners. His coming was unheralded and unknown to
any. During the summer months he made his home
in a dug-out in a deep ravine to the north of
the hill. Before the winter came he constructed him
a rude log-cabin, just to the east and near where the
parsonage now stands. Here he lived many years
leading the life of a recluse, and so retired from the
world and the rest of mankind that the people in
the neighborhood gave him the name of Hermit of
the Hill. None molested him in the least, but on
the contrary all seemed to fear and avoid him. His
long residence there was the source of a new name to
the hill. Shortly after his advent it was called
HERMIT HILL. For a time this name was most
common in use by all outside the pale of the Catholic
church, the members of which still adhered to the
name by which it had been christened by Father
Hasselbauer. A more extended account of the life

and adventures of this wandering and strange misanthrope will be found in another chapter and under the heading of "The Hermit of the Hill."

In later years a very important circumstance, in connection with the hill, took place giving rise to a new name, that of GOVERNMENT HILL. This name however never came into general use, but was confined principally to scientists who were engaged in work for the government.

In the summer of 1873 a corps of United States engineers took possession of the hill and erected on the summit a high observatory or signal station. They were sent out by the government to make a "lake survey" for the War Department at Washington. By it the coast line of lake Michigan was correctly defined and mapped out, showing clearly every harbor, bay, inlet, coast depression, high bluff, and promontory. The altitudes above the lake's level along the coast line were all carefully noted down and also the depth or shoal of water near its margin. By this method, of signaling from high inland points, it is claimed much better results can be obtained than by the old and uncertain way of meandering along the coast line.

Their tower was simply a tripod, three tall tamarack poles forming the legs. The point of observation was a small platform, twenty-five feet above the ground, from the centre of which a signal staff arose twenty-five feet, making the point of signal fifty feet above the base of tower. Directly below the signal staff a stone monument was set, the top being on a level with the ground. It is a lime stone, dressed, two feet in length and seven inches square. The top is smooth and in its centre is drilled an inch hole which is filled with lead. The letters U. S., are sunken in the surface, one on each side of the lead centre, and on a line due east and west. The monument is still in its original position, though now thirty inches below the surface, having been covered when the hill was graded for the new church. Its exact location may be determined by the following measurements: it stands about fourteen feet south of the church, fifteen feet in a southeasterly direction from the centre of the doorway and at a point where two lines cross each other, one drawn sixteen feet in a direction southwest from the southeast corner of the church, and the other thirty-three feet, in a direction southeast from the southwest corner, each line measuring from the inside corner of the brick abutments.

A second survey by government employes was made in 1881, and the same monument was used as a base for their operation. This survey was made for the Treasury Department, and was called the "lake survey." It was made for the purpose of establishing base lines between points on the Mississippi river and points on lakes Michigan and Superior.

During the present season, 1891, another corps of engineers was sent out from Washington to make a third survey. They came in the month of June and commenced their work on the hill from the old stone monument, which they unearthed without much trouble. They also erected a new signal tower to the northwest of the church. This was a "topographical survey," and made for the Department of the Interior. From this survey topographical maps are made showing the surface of the state. These maps are made forty inches square, on a scale of two miles to the inch, and are without reference to cities, towns or railroads; showing only the ground surface and location of hills, valleys, lakes, rivers, forests, prairies and marshes.

As the government has made use of the hill by making it a base for surveys extending through a period of nearly twenty years, and has established a permanent monument there as a reference or starting point for future surveys, it is quite natural that those engaged in the work should allude to it as the GOVERNMENT HILL.

As to the name by which the hill is now widely known and called, the author of this work claims the credit, if any there is, in having first introduced it to the public. When his poem of the Hermit was written in 1881, in looking around for a suitable name by which to entitle it, he hit upon a very significant alliteration, and called it the "Hermit of Holy Hill." This was chosen, not only as being applicable, but for the further reason, that it was harmonious and rythmical in sound.

It was not long after the poem made its first appearance in print, that many in the vicinity, when alluding to the hill, would drop the first two words of the poem's title, and using only the latter two, would call it, HOLY HILL. From that time the new title seemed to grow in favor, and among all classes near or far, no matter what their nationality was, or what their religious views might be, the name was, by common consent, universally accepted as being eminently proper, and was adopted by all, and in all likelihood never again to be changed. Indeed, what fitter or more appropriate name could be ascribed to the place? The words articulate with smoothness and with ease; they fall upon the ear of the hearer with the harmony and cadence of a well timed tune. They define and impress upon the mind that solemnity which pervades the hallowed domain, reminding one of the blessed sancity that lingers around and within the sacred enclosure.

Holy Hill—May its hallowed name, sacred and endeared to the present living, be forever perpetuated and transmitted to all future generations, unchanged by none; but sacredly preserved, even as its pristine and rural beauties are guarded and cherished by the living of to-day.

ST. MARY'S CHURCH ON HOLY HILL.

CHURCH HISTORY.

REV. J. B. HASSELBAUER.

WITH the historical part of the Catholic church, pertaining to Holy Hill, this chapter is especially devoted. In tracing its rise and progress for the past forty years, it is deemed proper to begin with the wonderful prediction made by Father Paulhuber nearly forty years ago, and which is quoted on page forty-six of this work. We say wonderful, because time with its ceaseless mutations has wrought out and fully demonstrated the truth of his prophecy. Whether it was by inspiration, or through conception of his own mind, that he foresaw the future greatness and renown that would attach to the hill in later years is now a thing unknown; yet certain it is, he so proclaimed it, and at a time when there was apparently nothing to indicate the great notoriety to which it has attained through the years that followed.

Just at what time the Rev. Paulhuber donated
the hill property to the church and took his departure for his home in the old country is not now
definitely known, but is supposed to have been in the
fall of 1856, the next year after he purchased the hill
from the government. This supposition is based
upon the fact, that Rev. J. B. Hasselbauer, who was
his immediate successor, had charge of the Richfield
parishes in 1857; hence, the time given must be
approximately correct.

Soon after assuming the charge of the parishes
above referred to, Reverend Hasselbauer gave
orders that a cross be erected on the summit of the
hill. Accordingly one was made by Roman Goetz at
the close of the year referred to. It was hewed from
a white oak tree that grew at the foot of the hill;
was five by seven inches in thickness, and when
erected stood fifteen feet above ground. The cross,
when finished, was carried by Mr. Goetz and his son-
in-law, Mathias Werner, to the top of the hill on
their shoulders, and placed in position.

The cross was solemnly blessed by Rev. Hasselbauer
in June 1858, who came over from St. Augustine's
church with a large procession for that purpose.
Soon after its dedication Roman Goetz made a
strong box from hard wood and fastened it securely
to the cross. It was kept locked, but was provided
with an opening in front large enough to allow the
deposit of a silver dollar. This was for the convenience of worshippers and pilgrims who might wish
to deposit a small offering when visiting the place.

Though the box was originally intended for only
small donations, still it was quite a revenue to the

church at times, as frequently large sums were deposited by devotees to the hill. In 1880, one Joseph Lang of Cleveland, Ohio, a nephew of Christian Lang, ex-county treasurer of Washington county, while worshipping at the hill, deposited in the box ninety-five dollars by way of donation. This is the largest amount ever deposited at any one time by a single individual, though larger amounts have in other ways been donated to the church by different persons in times past.

The old cross is still standing on the hill, near and to the south of the church. It is shown later on in this chapter in the cut illustrating the "Bell-tower and Cross." It is somewhat blemished and weather-beaten with age, and, as can be seen by the picture, shows signs of decay; and well it may, for in its exposed location it has withstood the fierce storms of time and has been subject to all the extremes of heat and cold for thirty-three years. It has outlasted the hand that fashioned it; the man who made and assisted in erecting it as an emblem of the sufferings of our Savior, upon the highest elevation of Holy Hill—Romanus Goetz—who died at the house of his son, Daniel at the foot of the hill, to the east, April 14th, 1891, at the age of eighty-six years. Romanus Goetz was foremost among the laymen of the Catholic church in the early history of the hill, and did much to advance its popularity. In the preceding chapter it will be seen that his name is first in the deed of 1876 from Washington County to the trustees of St. Mary's Chapel in the town of Erin. He was long the local custodian of the property, and took great pains to guard and preserve it from

molestation by any maliciously inclined. His valued
services to the church, before age made him retire
from active life, will long be remembered by the older
members, as will his friendly and civil traits to
strangers who have had occasion to visit the place
in times past.

The quaint and picturesque cottage of old Roman
Goetz is still standing at the foot of the hill, near to
the edge of the highway and opposite the entrance
to the bye-road leading up to the hill. A view of
this romantic and ancient land-mark is given on
page forty-three. The cottage is built from logs
hewn on both sides, chinked and pointed with plaster
inside and out. Its steep gables are shingled and
the roof to the south projects several feet beyond the
main part, forming a balcony or portico which is
boarded up and down. A pair of stairs starting
from the ground leads up into the dormitory. In the
balcony is a small window made at such a height
that a person standing and looking south will have
the church property directly before him. From this
commanding position the entrance to the grounds
and the church are plainly seen, as is, also, a portion
of the pathway leading to the top of the hill.

A rude picket-fence in front and a rail fence on the
sides and rear enclose the cottage. Tall elms of
native growth at the rear spread out their long
branches high above the cottage roof. In former
years this humble home did service as a hotel, where
hundreds of strangers yearly rested from their tiresome journeys, and satisfied their hunger at the
plain but hospitable board of Roman Goetz. His
name will long live in grateful remembrance along

side of those who, like Joseph Kohler, his sons and others, were ever foremost and ready in promoting the interest of their church and the popularity of Holy Hill.

Father Hasselbauer continued to minister to the parishes in Richfield and oversee the hill property until relieved by his successor, Rev. George Strickner, in the year of 1861. It is reported that he died several years ago, but the time or place of his death is not known to the writer. He is highly spoken of by those of his congregation who are still living, as a priest who had the respect and co-operation of every member of the church in the fields of his ministerial labors. His name will long be associated with the early history of the church, from the fact of his having blessed the cross and held the first divine services on Holy Hill.

COTTAGE HOME OF ROMAN GOETZ.

SEE ILLUSTRATION PAGE 43.

--

(FROM THE HERMIT OF HOLY HILL.)

When pilgrims trav'ling to the shrine
  Approach the spot where christians wait,
They pass the highway's steep decline
  And halt before the rustic gate.

Here on the hillside, standing near
  The winding highway's rugged bend,
Is seen a cottage, quaint and queer,
  With stairway on its outer end.

'Tis built from logs, each hewn with care;
  Its shingled gables, deftly laid;
With balcony above the stair,
  In rude simplicity is made.

One window on its southern side—
A sort of look-out, if you will—
Takes in the landscape far and wide,
And keeps a guard o'er Holy Hill.

The vine-clad walls, that half conceal
  The entrance to this rural cot,
Doth lend a charm that makes one feel
  As loth to leave this rustic spot.

Here elms of ancient growth outspread
  Their old fantastic boughs on high,
And weave a second roof o'er head,
  Betwixt the cottage and the sky.

Built in its rude and rustic way—
  True copy of the Alpine cot—
A haven and a home, they say,
  Who chance this wild secluded spot.

Here dwelt old Roman Goetz, long years
  The guard and guide to Holy Hill;
This was his home, and as appears,
  Where all were greeted with good-will.

For Roman's welcome free from guile,
  As sanctioned by his proffered hand,
Made many a weary pilgrim smile,
  And feel at home in stranger land.

None came that way but halted here—
He held the Chapel's iron key,
Yet all in welcome worshipped there,
And with his kind approval free.

His cottage old and rude still stands,
   Near to the winding highway's edge,
Where many a weary traveler lands,
   To rest him from his pilgrimage.

But Roman Goetz, the man of worth,
   No longer bids the pilgrim rest;
But sleeping with the good of earth,
   His soul's reward is with the blest.

SHRINE BY THE WAY-SIDE.

CHURCH HISTORY.

Rev. George Strickner succeeded Father Hasselbauer to the pastorate of the churches of
St. Boniface and St. Augustine in Richfield in 1861.
When assuming the charge of those parishes the care
and protection of the hill property were also assigned
to him. About this time a number of the members
of St. Augustine's congregation, especially those
residing near the hill, conceived the plan of building
a little chapel for worship on the hill near the cross.
They laid their plans before Father Strickner, who,
not only sanctioned their request, but gave them
encouragement in aid of their undertaking.

Work on the little chapel was begun in the summer
of 1862. Though the church as contemplated, was
simply a small structure, yet to build it was quite an

undertaking owing to the difficulty in getting the material up the steep and rough hillside; and the succeeding winter had nearly passed away before all the material was on the ground. It was built of logs smoothly hewn on two sides, and were all made the same length, as the building was to be just sixteen feet square. The timbers were cut and all prepared ready for laying, down at the bottom of the hill. To get them to the place required much time and a vast amount of hard labor. They were first hauled about halfway up with a team, to a level spot at the upper end of the ravine. From there, resting on levers, they were carried up the rest of the way by hand.

On Good Friday, 1863, the little chapel on Holy Hill was raised, the people coming from far and near to assist in the work. It did not take long to complete the building and get it ready for dedication. On the twenty-fourth day of May, 1863, being the Titular Feast of the church and termed "Feast of St. Mary's help of Christians," Rev. George Strickner blessed the chapel with solemn ceremonies. On that day the first sermon on Holy Hill was preached to an audience numbering, at least fifteen hundred persons. It was delivered from the step in front of the door, the immense congregation standing densely covering the entire summit of the hill.

The little chapel was sixteen feet square, stood on a stone foundation and fronted to the west. Its stone walls had an elevation of about twelve feet higher than that of the new church; that much of the top of the hill having been graded down when the foundation for the new church was laid. The

exact location of the old chapel was nearly the same
as that now occupied by the sacristy of the new
church. On the outside it was about ten feet high
from the ground to eaves, and on the inside some
eight feet between floor and ceiling. It contained a
door, to the west, and four windows, two at the
north and two on the south side. The inside walls
were painted and plastered, as was the ceiling overhead. The interior contained a rude altar, neatly
covered, and on which were arranged various
articles, such as are generally used in Catholic places
of worship. The walls were adorned with pictures
and charts illustrative and commemorative of events
in the history of the christian religion. In the southwest corner stood a number of crutches and above
them hung several other tokens of diseases, which
had been left there, as evidence of cures, by those
who had been relieved of their afflictions through
the potent, yet inscrutable efficacy of earnest and
sincere prayer. A bench in front of the altar and
one at each side of the building, a brass vessel for
holding holy water and box for offerings completed
the inner outfit of the chapel.

On the exterior, over the door, was fastened an
image of Christ upon the Cross. It was about one-
third life size, and the same one that is represented on
page seventy-three in the cut entitled, "a shrine by
the wayside." The exterior walls, from the base to a
height as far as could be reached, were cut and carved
with dates and names, until not a single space on
either of the four walls was left large enough, even
for a monogram.

It must be a strange motive or infatuation that

prompts one to commit a misdemeanor of this kind; a crime in the nature of sacrilege as defined by our laws, by defacing a place of public worship. He, who does this, considers but little, that aside from laying himself liable to a fine and imprisonment, he is carving his name where it will stand as a monument of his egotism and his lasting shame and disgrace.

Rev. George Strickner continued as priest of the Richfield parishes and custodian of the hill property for about ten years, or until 1870. He has long since retired from the ministry and is now living at Sheboygan, Wisconsin. He was a man of fine scholarly attainments, social and entertaining to all who formed his acquaintance. His old parishioners still speak highly of him as a paternal friend and spiritual adviser.

BELL TOWER AND CROSS.

HOLY HILL was under the direct charge of the priests who officiated at St. Hubert's parish, from the time of its purchase by Father Paulhuber in May, 1855, to the year of 1883, when it passed to the keeping of Rev. N. M. Zimmer, pastor of the Hartford congregation, and in whose custody it has since remained.

Of the many priests who had charge of the property during that interval of thirty years, only a few figured prominently in its history or were connected with its improvements. But, as a matter of history, and to show who have had charge of the property since its purchase from Government to the present time, we give the names of the officiating priests and their approximate terms of service.

At the time when Father Paulhuber purchased the property, St. Hubert's congregation was in charge of Rev. M. Peiffer, who officiated until the

spring of 1856. His successor was Rev. F. B. Hasselbauer whose term lasted to August, 1859. Then
followed two very short terms, first by Rev. B. Weik-
mann, from August, 1859 till January, 1860, and
second by Rev. M. Heiss to June, 1861. These are now
all dead, the last named, Rev. Heiss, having died as
pastor of St. Andrew's church, at Le Roy, Dodge Co.,
in July of 1890. Rev. George Strickner followed as
pastor from June, 1861 to 1865. Rev. Francis Spath,
who died while pastor of the Sehleisingerville
church, September 17, 1890, succeeded Rev. Strickner but officiated only on a few occasions.

Rev. A. Foeckler succeeded Father Spath from the
fall of 1865 to March 1867. Rev. Foeckler died at
Racine in the fall of 1889. Rev. John Gamber was
then pastor from March, 1867 to 1870. He, also, has
died. Rev. A. Michels then officiated for one year,
closing with January, 1871. Rev. Michels is now
chaplain of Greenfield Park Convent, Milwaukee Co.
His successor was Rev. J. H. Korfhage, who continued to January, 1872, and who is now chaplain
and pastor near Jefferson, Wisconsin.

Rev. John Welter now filled the place till May,
1875. Rev. Welter, after leaving St. Hubert's church
officiated for a short time at Paris, Kenosha county,
where his failing health finally compelled him to
resign his charge. He died in the city of Kenosha
in the year of 1877, and was buried at Holy Cross,
Ozaukee Co. His successor was Reverend Ferdinand
Racss, who was pastor from May, 1875 to the fall
of 1883, at which time the custodianship of the hill
property was passed to the Rev. N. M. Zimmer,
pastor of St. Kilian's church at Hartford.

During the time that Rev. Ferdinand Raess had charge of St. Hubert's church, extending through a term of eight years, the church records show that at various times Revs. A. Ambauer, L. Beck and Dominicus, Capuchin Father, of the order of St. Francis, held services there. As the custody of Holy Hill passed from St. Hubert's church with the ending of the pastorate of Father Raess, it is only necessary to add that the intervening time has been filled by the Rev. gentlemen in the following order: Capuchin Father and Rev. Peter Frieden from 1883 to 1884; by Rev. August Albers, from 1884 to 1886; by Rev. A. F. Schinners from 1886 to 1887, and by Rev. B. Weyer, from 1887 to June, 1890, since which date the church has been, and now is, presided over by the Rev. N. J. Nickel, and to whom we are greatly indebted for much of the information contained in this chapter.

It is stated on the authority of Rev. N. M. Zimmer, that all of the Rev. Fathers mentioned above prior to Rev. John Welter, resided at St. Boniface, and only attended St. Hubert's and St. Augustine's as out-missions. Rev. John Welter was the first priest to reside at St. Hubert's church. Rev. Paulhuber resided at St. Boniface when he purchased the Holy Hill property.

THE time when Father Raess assumed charge
of St. Hubert's church marks the beginning of
the rise which culminated in the distinguished prominence to which Holy Hill has attained. He it was,
who seemingly foresaw for the future that which had
been prophesied by Father Paulhuber twenty years
previous to his time; and well and ardently, for years,
did he labor that the wonderful prediction might be
fully verified. Time has demonstrated that his labor
was not in vain.

During the time he had charge of the property he
not only encouraged, but generously contributed to,
many of the lasting improvements that now adorn
that noted and sacred place of worship. During his
custodianship the roadway leading from below to
the summit of the hill was graded so as to allow
teams to ascend and descend with comparative ease
and safety. He witnessed the planting of the first

Stations by the side of the beautiful and romantic pathway. He sanctioned the removal of the "little chapel on the hill;" the ground upon which it stood to be leveled; he saw in its place rise the grand edifice which now ornaments its summit, and he took part in the ceremonies at its dedication.

REVEREND FERDINAND RAESS was born at Glaris, Glarus county, Switzerland, on the 31st day of January, 1831. He received his early education in a gymnasium school presided over by Benedictine Father of Disentis, at Grison. He afterwards attended the Episcopal seminary at Chur, and where he completed his course of education and graduated in the studies of philosophy and theology. He was ordained a priest at Chur, County of Grison, by Bishop "Von Carl," on the third day of August, 1856, and soon afterwards entered upon his priestly duties and performed clerical work in the old conntry for about eleven years.

In 1867 he immigrated to this country, landing in the city of New York on the 27th day of July of that year. On his arrival in this country he assumed charge of a parish at Ellenville, in the state of New York, which he continued to 1871. He then went to Covington, Kentucky, where he officiated as a priest until 1873. He then came to Wisconsin and took charge of a congregation at Manitowoc. He remained there until he assumed charge of the parishes of St. Hubert and St. Augustine in Richfield, April 9th, 1875, with residence at the former place. He was pastor of those congregations until September 1883, serving a longer term than any before him or since. After leaving St. Hubert's the author is uncertain as

to where he passed the next succeeding five years of
his life. However, we know he assumed charge of the
parish at New Berlin, Waukesha county and entered
upon his duties there, July 3rd, 1888. He continued
as pastor of that parish until the present year, and
is now the priest of a congregation at Kieler, Grant
county, Wisconsin.

Father Raess must have been possessed of a most
wonderful fund of force, energy and executive ability,
for while ministering to the spiritual wants of two
separate congregations, he still managed to find
time to superintend the manifold improvements that
were constantly going on at the Hill during his eight
year term of service. These improvements were
many and some of them quite expensive, requiring
a large outlay of money to meet the constant
demands for labor and materials; and, with not an
overstocked treasury, to meet these requirements
was a task of no small importance. It is a matter
of record that during those eight years he traveled
far and over a wide extent of country, visiting numerous parishes and was quite successful in soliciting
aid by way of donations which was used to carry on
and complete the works which he had undertaken.

His first noteworthy act was in correcting the
imperfect title to the property, and subsequently by
having the title transferred from the trustees of St.
Mary's chapel of Erin, to the most Rev. John Martin
Henni, archbishop of the Milwaukee diocese. This
transfer, brought about at his personal instance and
request, was consummated May 26, 1876, the next
year after the keeping of the property had been dele-
gated to him.

Rev. Ferd. Raess

Two years later a very important and attractive feature was added to the Hill. This was by establishing "the way of the Cross," and erecting the first stations by the pathway. It is not positively certain that Father Raess was the prime mover in this improvement, yet certain it is that the work was done during his custodianship, and consequently must have been done with his knowledge and approval. It is stated, and on good authority, that the first "stations of the Cross" were established at the suggestion or by request of the Rev. Dominicus, Capuchin Father, and were blessed by him in the year 1878.

These stations, which were simply crosses, were made by George Klippel of Richfield. They were not of the most durable kind, being made from pine, about six inches wide, four inches in thickness and stood about eight feet high above ground. The top and ends of the arms were ornamented in resemblance of a clover leaf, conforming to the accepted pattern of the Roman Cross. In the center square, where the arms crossed the upright, was fastened a picture, each one commemorative of some scene or act in the trial, sentence and crucifixion of Christ. Below, and in front of each station, was placed a low stool or bench on which pilgrims knelt to pray while making the "stations of the Cross."

Most of the old stations had different locations from those now occupied by the present ones. Old station number ten, is shown on page 73, standing at the left in the cut of the "shrine by the way side." This little shrine or chapel, was built in the spring of 1879, and made as a depository and for the safe

keeping of such articles of worship as were contained
in the old log chapel on the hill, and which was torn
down to give place for the new church which was
then being built. By another writer on the history
of the Hill, this little shrine is illustrated and called
the "Hermit's Hut." This is a grave error, as the
shrine was built several years after the hermit had
departed from the place. It was taken down as soon
as the new church was so far completed as to offer
shelter and security for the church fixtures.

When the first stations were erected, in 1878, a
new pathway was laid out from below to the top of
the hill, along which the stations were placed. The
new route deviated somewhat from the old one,
being farther to the west and traversed the high
ground from the beginning. The old and new pathway met just a few feet north of where the new
station, number nine, now stands. The following
year Father Raess caused the new route to be graded
as a roadway, to facilitate the getting of materials
up the hill for the new church which was commenced
in 1879.

Prior to the time when Father Raess took charge
of the property, the Hill had gained but little more
than a local celebrity. It was, however, well pat-
ronized by the members of neighboring parishes on
all regular "feast days." During the pleasant summer season, might be seen there, many stranger
pilgrims, who came to worship in solitude. Also,
one might see there many who were bowed down
with afflictions from various diseases who were seeking relief through hope, faith and prayer.

With the advent of Father Raess the Hill began

to assume an air of prominence and popularity, and has continued to grow in popular favor with each succeeding year, until now it stands without a rival of its kind anywhere upon this continent. On all regular "feast days" the people that congregate there are numbered by thousands. They come from long distances, and on such occasions nearly every city in the state is represented. During the summer season thousands of strangers from different states and countries visit this noted place. Some are simple tourists seeking pleasure amid these rural haunts; others are led there merely to gratify a sensitive or morbid curiosity; but by far the greater number of visitors are pilgrims and religious devotees who come to worship in solitude and do homage at the sacred shrine of Mary.

The stations are fourteen in number, and are distributed at regular intervals along the pathway from the entrance to the grounds to the church on the hill-top. This whole pilgrimage, which is eighteen hundred and sixty-two feet in length, has been fairly graded for pedestrians, and is frequently used as a carriage-way, though not with any degree of safety. It meanders the hill by a circuitous route and up the steep ascent to the summit where it reaches an altitude of two hundred and sixty feet above the gateway.

The entire pathway leads through a dense forest which is still standing in all its original beauty and pristine grandeur. A deep gloom, even at mid-day, over-shadows its whole extent, causing a sense of loneliness and profound sanctity to take possession of all who tread this sacred domain.

When one has passed through the gateway and
stands before station one, by some strange and
unseen agency, the sacredness of the place suddenly
becomes manifest. He is at once deeply impressed
with the mysterious solemnity everywhere present.
This sense of feeling comes to all who sojourn within
that sacred enclosure, and most reverently do all
respect and comply with the divine attribute. This
is invariably so, whether they are professors of
christianity, unbelievers or atheists.

Watch the long procession of devotees as they
move slowly and solemnly onward from station to
station, and you will see no sign of levity or mirth
reflected on the features of any. All worship with
that calm serenity and meek devotion known only
to the true followers of Christ. Witnessing this, the
most stoic infidel must be obdurate indeed if he is
not influenced to seriousness and compassion by the
solemnity which surrounds him.

Most wonderful pilgrimage! How matchlessly
grand, amidst thy sylvan groves, God's temples!
How intensly charming surrounded by thy rural
beauties! This most worshipful stretch of solitude,
where every soul might hide himself away with God
and be invisible to all save those to whom he would
reveal himself.

THE PILGRIMAGE.

(FROM THE HERMIT OF HOLY HILL.)

Where forests as ancient as Time in its race,
Surround Holy Hill from its summit to base;
In the shade of that wildwood, gloomy and deep,
One lone narrow pathway meanders the steep.

Up the steep hillside with brambles o'er grown,
And through the dark valley, deserted and lone,
Still onward it winds to the hill's highest crest,
The goal of the pilgrim—the shrine of the blest.

Worn is the pathway where christians have trod
For years in this solitude, worshipping God;
No place is more sacred, none more opportune,
Where man with his Saviour alone can commune.

Along this steep pathway, and through the defile,
There you meet hundreds, but never a smile
Can be seen on the faces of pilgrims who go,
Toiling with steps that are measured and slow.

Still onward and upward with sanctified air—
Now kneeling at stations they offer their prayer;
Prayers to the Virgin, and prayers to her Son,
Who hath died for our sins—the Crucified One.

All solemn they move—the path where they tread
Is moist from the tears by the penitents shed;
Whilst a halo of brightness illumes their dark way,
Where forests have shut out the sunlight of day.

Here you meet pilgrims who hail from afar,
Beaconed and guided by MARY, the star!
Bright radient star of the infinite sea,
Whose broad waters reach out to eternity.

The faithful comply with Her righteous behest;
Inspired they follow the cross on the crest—
That emblem of christians—His banner unfurled,
Shines bright o'er the hill-top, a light to the world.

Some in the strength of their manhood are there—
The maid and the matron the pilgrimage share;
Whilst many, whose tottering footsteps betray
The sad burdens of life, have met here to pray.

The sightless are groping their way in the dark;
And those with the seal of infirmity's mark—
Forms that are bowed with affliction you meet,
Who for worship have come to this sacred retreat.

Here you find mingling the high with the low,
The rich with the child of misfortune and woe.
All meet on one level, they seek but to win
Salvation of soul through redemption from sin.

They kneel at one altar, they worship but One;
For in unit are SPIRIT, the FATHER and SON:
Relief from life's burdens, they ask and implore—
Belief and repentance, through prayer can restore

Faith in the promise of Him who hath said—
"Believe thou in me, and though ye are dead,
Yet shall ye live," and His promise Divine,
Brings comfort to all who kneel at His shrine.

As the patronage of the Hill gradually increased with each succeeding year Father Raess early saw the necessity of having a more commodious place for worship than that afforded by the little log chapel. He, therefore, conceived the idea of building a church of dimensions suitable to accommodate the thousands that assembled there on all especial days of worship. Accordingly, early in the winter of 1879, he communicated his purpose to the most Rev. Archbishop Henni, who not only approved of the undertaking suggested, but also offered him aid in the prosecution of the contemplated improvement.

Thus encouraged, he next applied to architect H. C. Koch of Milwaukee, who, for one hundred dollars, furnished him with the plans and specifications, together with estimated cost of the improvements designed. It was yet in mid-winter when the plans were finished and approved, and Father Raess lost no time in getting everything in readiness to commence building the church early in the spring.

The specifications called for two hundred thousand bricks and to obtain these was the most serious problem that presented itself in the way of building. No bricks were made nearer than Schleisingerville, seven miles distant, and the road between there and the Hill was rough and very hilly. To overcome this obstacle Father Raess consulted an experienced brickmaker, one John Rover of Sheboygan, to ascertain if bricks might not be made in the vicinity of the Hill. He was told by him, if a quantity of suitable clay could be found anywhere in that neighborhood there would be no difficulty, as there was plenty of good sand in the range of hills, and he promised to prospect for clay as soon as the ground would permit. Accordingly, he came early in the spring and made an examination of the soil at various points adjacent to the hill. Fortunately a bed of good clay was found about sixty rods north of the northeast corner of the hill property. Here he at once commenced the work of making bricks for the church, which when burned were found to be of an excellent quality. The debris, showing the location of the kilns where the bricks were made, can still be plainly seen just to the left of, and a few rods after leaving, the highway for the Hill.

The frost had barely left the ground in the spring of 1879, when a large force of men were set at work grading down the top of the hill and leveling a space sufficiently large for the foundation of the new church and for the convenience of building. It is estimated that the hill was lowered some seven feet from its original height before the level space was brought down to the required size.

By a peculiar formation of the hill the ground thus leveled would not permit of standing the church in a true line with the primary points of compass. Therefore, to accommodate its size to the situation it was located fronting nearly south, with its sides extending from the front corners twenty-three degrees east from a line running due north and south.

Getting the materials for building up the steep hill was another serious difficulty and must have involved quite an expense, when we consider, as stated, that two hundred bricks were accounted a sufficient load for an ordinary team to haul up the hill. Fortunately, enough stones for the foundation were procured by leveling down the hill, but to get all other needed material on the ground was no inexpensive or light task.

The contract for doing the work was let to John Fellenz of Milwaukee for five thousand dollars and was built in accordance with the original plan as furnished by architect Koch. It has an extreme length of seventy feet, with extension for altar, and a width of forty-six feet, with an annex at the north-east corner for a sacristy, eighteen feet square. The walls are twenty feet high to the eaves, are solid brick and iron-anchored to the heavy stone foundation. The roof is steep, and above it rises the steeple surmounted with a gilt cross the top of which has an elevation of sixty-eight feet above the stone water table. Each of the corners and side walls are doubly strengthened with heavy brick buttresses extending from the stone foundation to the cap or cornice.

The church is lighted with fourteen high Gothic windows, five on each side and two each, at the rear and front. It also has two circular windows one in each gable, the one in front being located directly above the high arched doorway. The glass in the windows is stained a variety of colors and is ornamented and so arranged as to produce a most pleasing effect.

The corner stone, which was not placed in position until June, is located in the southwest corner and about three feet above the ground. It is a dressed lime stone, about one foot in thickness and twenty inches square. On its south exposed surface is the inscription—"ERECTED 1879," the letters and numerals being deeply sunken in the face. The water table, window and door sills and coppings of the buttresses are made from dressed lime stone.

The ground on both sides of the church and in the rear has been evenly graded, leaving a fine promenade, from ten to fifteen feet wide on each side, and twenty-five feet in the rear to the north. This point is the grand observatory, and where all who visit the hill love to linger long in viewing the beautiful panorama spread out far below and around them. A small amount of money and labor might be profitably expended in leveling up and beautifying the ground in front of the church, and which, undoubtedly will ere long be done.

Owing to the many difficulties, causing frequent and long delays, the work of building progressed slowly. During the winter season the work was entirely suspended, and it was not until three summers had nearly passed away that the church was so far completed as to be ready for dedication. At length all was in readiness, and on a beautiful autumn day,

September eighth, 1881, in the presence of a vast assemblage, the church was blessed with solemn ceremonies by the most Rev. Arch-bishop Heiss. On this solemn occasion the new church was christened. *St. Mary's Auxilium Christianorum*, or St. Mary's Help of Christians.

Father Raess lived to enjoy the satisfaction of seeing the new church completed under his personal management, or at least so far as to afford an acceptable and commodious place of worship for its constantly increasing patronage. Most assuredly, it must have been a source of great pleasure to one, who for three long years, had labored so assiduously to accomplish such a grand undertaking. For the next two years succeeding the dedication of the new church Father Raess resided at the hill and presided over its welfare, and where he had the pleasure of noting its growing prosperity and popularity.

Soon after the work on the new church had been commenced, Father Raess removed from St. Hubert's parish in Richfield, and took up his residence in the old Swiss cottage belonging to Roman Goetz, in order to be nearer to the work in which he was then engaged. Without doubt, it was this change in residence that first suggested to him the propriety of building a parsonage in connection with the new church. This conclusion is reached from the fact that, shortly after his change of residence, we find him laying plans for the erection of a new parsonage on the premises and convenient to the church then building.

The place which he chose for its location was in the deep ravine at the foot of the hill to the north; a very secluded and picturesque spot. In fact, it was nearly identical with the one chosen by the hermit, and near which his log hut was built some fifteen years previously. The hermit's abode, though then untenanted, was still standing; but it was burned down the same summer that the church and parsonage were begun. The cause of its burning has always remained a profound secret and mystery, though by some it has been intimated that the rude hovel was set on fire by one of the workmen engaged on the church. At all events, it was quite natural that its uncouth presence could not long be tolerated there and especially by the side of so stately a building soon to take its place.

Father Raess had fully decided to build the new parsonage as early as 1879, the same season the church was commenced, though nothing was done towards it that summer further than selecting a site and letting of some contracts. John Fellenz, who had the contract for building the church, was also awarded the contract for doing the work on the parsonage for one thousand dollars. The matter of purchasing all necessary materials Father Raess reserved for himself. It was not finished and ready for occupancy until late in the fall of 1880.

The parsonage is built in the modern style of architecture and is, altogether a very imposing structure. It is three stories high and has a frontage to the south of twenty-eight feet, with a width of twenty-six feet. The first or lower story is built of stone and serves mainly for a kitchen, dining room, pantry and cellar. The two upper stories are wood, the second being provided with a spacious parlor or sitting-room, a study, bedroom and closet. From this a door opens into a hall with a stair leading to the upper story, which is divided up into several sleeping rooms. A wide veranda extends across the entire front, its floor being on a level with that of the second story. This is reached from the inside by a door opening out from the sitting room, and from the outside by a stair leading up from the ground in front. See page 151.

A fine view may be had from the veranda looking in any direction one may. Directly before you, to the south, at a distance of not more than six rods, the hill begins its steep ascent. The side presented to view is covered with a dense forest extending upward to the very summit; while far up on the hilltop, above the highest foliage, are seen the roof and steeple to the church, and above all, the bright gilded cross glitters against the sky like the sun's rays reflected from the still surface of some tranquil lake. To the east, through the deep gorge, extends a beautiful, smooth, narrow lawn, in which are growing a number of vigorous looking fruit trees. Above their tops, which are far below the level on which you stand, away in the distance are seen the fruitful fields of husbandry. Looking west, the hill rises up just before you, almost perpendicularly, to a height of sixty feet until it meets the graded pathway leading to the summit of the hill. From here one can trace its meandering course for quite a distance in either direction. At this point four of the fourteen stations can be readily observed, a greater number than can be seen at one time from any other one point on the whole hill.

Father Raess took possession of the new parsonage in October, 1880, and continued to reside there until September, 1883, at which time he relinquished his custodianship of the Holy Hill property. Since he vacated the parsonage it has never been occupied as a residence by any one, and perhaps, never will be again, for it is conceded by nearly all, that as a place for solitary devotion, and as a pilgrimage where solitude is an essential element, the place loses the greater part of its charm and solemnity by having a human abode inhabited within its sacred precincts.

Father Raess performed a great and good mission, and retired from his field of labor with the respect and good will of all with whom he had any dealings. The extent of his labor, during the last four years he had charge of the hill, is told by the recorded fact, that he expended the aggregate sum of ten thousand and nine hundred dollars for the improvements on Holy Hill. To meet the payment of the expenses incurred, he received from the most Rev. M. Heiss, five thousand dollars. The balance, five thousand and nine hundred dollars was made up by donations and from his own money, the latter portion being by far the largest amount.

HAT credit which is due and conceded to Father Raess for his valued services and munificent donations, which have contributed so largely to the popularity of Holy Hill, is likewise justly due and accorded to his eminent successor, the Rev. Father Zimmer. Fortunate, it was, for the present and future greatness of the Hill, that the custody of the property passed immediately after Father Raess, to one who has exercised so much care in preserving and completing the many improvements begun by his most worthy predecessor. During the many years that Father Zimmer has had charge of the property, not one has passed by without something having been added in the way of improving and beautifying the place.

Like his predecessor, Father Zimmer, during his term of service, has had the care of ministering to the spiritual wants of two separate congregations, that of St. Kilian's in Hartford, and of St. Patrick's in Erin. He also, like Father Raess, has devoted the greater part of his spare time to the improvement of Holy Hill, in the management of which, his endeavor has been marked by the utmost energy, zeal and devotion. All his labors in this direction have been executed with precision and economy, and never in excess of the resources at his command.

One instance illustrative of his exact and systematic method of discharging the duties assigned to him, is noticed in the fact, that each year he prepares an annual statement, showing all the receipts and expenditures. These are printed on slips of paper and passed out to the congregation at the Titular feast of the church, which occurs on the twenty-fourth day of May, being the commencement of solemn services on Holy Hill in each year. For the benefit of those who may hereafter peruse this book, and that the unacquainted may have a better knowledge of the benign and courteous priest. whose personal efforts conduced so much to perpetuate the fame and celebrity of Holy Hill, the following brief biography is appended.

REVEREND NICHOLAS M. ZIMMER is the eldest son of John and Catharine, *nee* Friedrich, Zimmer, who emigrated from their native land, Rhenish Province, Germany, in 1847. Soon after their arrival in this country they purchased a farm near Menomonee Falls, Waukesha county, Wisconsin, and where Nicholas M., the present Rev. Father Zimmer, was born, January 10th, 1848. His parents continued to live upon the old homestead until 1873, at which time their son had charge of St. Alphonius church at

Rev. N. M. Zimmer

New Munster, when they transferred the farm to their youngest son and have since made their home with him. They are both still living, and though each has attained to the allotted age of human expectancy, yet notwithstanding their years both are still in the enjoyment of good health.

His early life and boyhood's days were passed at his parents' home, and did not differ materially from those usually known to boys brought up on a farm. He had his full share of incidents and accidents common to youth, some of which, at times, were of so severe and serious a nature as to endanger his young life. He received his first education in a parochial school at Fussville, to attend which he was obliged to travel three miles, morning and evening. It was at this place where he received his first holy communion when eleven years of age. He afterwards attended for two terms a public school which was taught near his own home. When fourteen years of age he entered St. Francis Seminary near Milwaukee, where he commenced and completed his course of classical and ecclesiastical studies.

At the age of twenty-two years and eleven months, on the seventeenth day of December 1870, he was ordained to the priesthood by the Rt. Rev. John Martin Henni. A noteworthy incident in his history is, that he said his first mass on the Christmas day following his ordination in St. Anthony's church in Fussville, being the same church in which he was baptized, and where he received his first holy communion and was confirmed.

It was on the first day of January 1871, that Rev. Father Zimmer received his first appointment,

as assistant priest to the Rev. Conrad, of Holy
Trinity church in Milwaukee, which position he
filled until May of the same year, when he was sent
to take charge of St. John's congregation at Paris,
Kenosha county. He remained there until June, 1872,
when he was called to take charge of St. Joseph's
parish at Grafton, Ozauke county, where he remained
to October of that year. From that time, and until
May 1874, he had charge of St. Alphonius' church at
New Munster, Kenosha county. He was then appointed as priest in charge of St. Francis church at
Lake Geneva, Walworth county, which has an Irish
congregation with a German outmission. He remained there until the eighth day of October 1883,
when he was called to the charge of St. Kilian's congregation at Hartford, and where he at present
resides.

Since his residence in Hartford, Father Zimmer,
aside from the clerical duties devolving upon him by
reason of the two congregations already mentioned,
has devoted a goodly share of his spare time in an
endeavor to promote and perpetuate the good name
of Holy Hill. His attention was early directed to
the proper observance of all regular feast-days that
occur during the season of divine service there. On
these occasions many priests from the neighboring
parishes, and frequently from long distances, by his
invitation congregate there to take part and assist
in the solemn ceremonies of the occasions.

At least two weeks previous to the days fixed
for such selomn observances, at his request, word is
given out of the event by the neighboring priests
in their respective churches. He also causes notice

to be published in the local papers, and even in some printed as far away as Milwaukee, giving the time and place, the name and religious meaning of each day of holy obligation.

So thoroughly and practically does he cause these notices to go out before the public that on these feast days the people flock to the Hill from near and far, and the multitude that gathers there can usually be numbered by the thousands. At such times, not only does one meet there people who come for miles around and from every direction, but also, are seen hundreds of strangers who have come from their homes in distant parts of the country.

There are five principal feast-days celebrated on Holy Hill during the summer of each year, and as a rule there may be six. These days are particularly described in their order in a subsequent chapter of this book. Besides these particular days of solemn services, there are other days set apart during the pleasant summer months for excursions which come by railroad from the larger cities. Also, congregations in the neighborhood surrounding the hill usually select one day for a private pilgrimage, and which is known only to the members of that particular congregation.

On excursion days the railroad trains usually stop at the Hartford station, the hill being reached from there better than from any other point on the road, it being somewhat nearer, a better road and the facilities of getting to and from the hill are far better than at any other station. Yet even at such times, when excursionists come by the hundreds, it requires considerable generalship on the part of

Father Zimmer to marshal a sufficient number of carriages to convey all comfortably to the hill.

It is not the intention of the author to follow here all the improvements made by Father Zimmer during his long custodianship of the hill. These will all be given in detail in a subsequent chapter. As the building of the new stations, or "Way of the Cross," was done under his direction, it is deemed proper at this place to take up the history of their origin, giving their use and application to the Catholic religion.

VIA CRUCIS, OR WAY OF THE CROSS.

No religious denomination, other than the Catholic, has so rigidly adhered to the ritual, observances and customs, established by their church from its very commencement and until down to the present time. From its earliest history, which originated with Christ and his Apostles, there has been but little or no change in its ceremonies or forms of worship for a space of time covering nearly two thousand years.

Among the many beautiful and impressive ceremonies that have remained sacredly unaltered through the long lapse of years is what is known as the "Way of the Cross," established to memorize the sentence, sufferings, death upon the Cross and burial of our Lord and Saviour, Jesus Christ. Perhaps in no other way could these memorable events be so vividly impressed and fixed upon the mind and memory as by this allegorical and figurative method. While reverently praying in the presence of these sacred mementoes surrounded by the reflections of ages past, the true and devout christian seems to live, for the time, in the presence of the Saviour of men, and contemporaneous with His persecutions and death.

The same feelings of compassion for Him who suffered and died upon the cross, and the same indignation towards His accusers and persecutors, are felt by those who reverently and sincerely make the Stations of the Cross to-day, as were known and felt by the followers of Christ who witnessed the Crucifixion on Mount Calvary. The semblance of the same scenes are reproduced in statuary; the same prayers are offered, and the *Stabat Mater*, without a word or syllable of alteration is still sung as when first composed in the Latin tongue by Jacoponi, who died in 1306. He was a Franciscan monk at the time of St. Francis Assissi. His proper name was Jacob De Benedictis.

The stations are fourteen in number, each one representing some particular event that transpired from the time Christ received his death sentence before Pilate, until his body was taken from the cross and laid in the sepulcher. They are distributed at intervals along the pathway leading from the entrance to the grounds, to the cross and church on the hill-top.

For the inscriptions, with their interpretation; the meditations enjoined upon Pilgrims; the *Stabat Mater* and general explanation of the Stations and their uses, we are indebted to a little volume published by H. L. Kliner & Co., with the approbation of the Most Rev. Patrick John, archbishop of Philadelphia, November 15th, 1889. They are given in the book as follows:

"Among those devotional exercises which have for their object meditation on the Passion, Cross and Death of our Lord and Saviour Jesus Christ, sovereign remedy for the conversion of sinners, for the renovation of the trepid, and for the sanctification of the just; one of the chief has ever been the exercises of the Way of Calvary called *via crucis.* This devotional exercise has continued in an unbroken tradition from the time of the crucifixion, when Christ ascended into Heaven, arose first in Jerusalem amongst the Christians who dwelt there. Out of veneration for those sacred spots which were sanctified by the sufferings of our Divine Redeemer; even from the very times of the Gospel, as we learn from St. Jerome, Christians were wont to visit the holy places in crowds; and there were gathering of all persons, he says, even from the farthest corners of the earth, to visit those holy places, and which continued down to his own times.

From Jerusalem this devout exercise was introduced into Europe by various pious and holy persons who had traveled to the Holy Land to satisfy their devotion. Amongst others, we read of the blessed Alvarez, of the order of Friars Preachers, who after he returned to his own convent of St. Dominic in Cordova, built several little chapels, in which, after the way of separate Stations, he had painted the principal events which took place on our Lord's way to Mount Calvary.

In later years observants of the order of St. Francis, as soon as the foundation of their Order was established, introduced them into the Holy Land; and more especially from the year of 1342, when they had their house in Jerusalem established, and had the custody of the sacred places; then, both in Italy and elsewhere, in fact, throughout the whole Catholic world, began to spread the devotion of the *via Crucis.*

This they effected by erecting in their own churches fourteen separate stations, in visiting which, it was said, that "the faithful, like the devout pilgrims who go in person to visit the holy places in Jerusalem, do themselves also make this journey in spirit, whilst they meditate on all that our Lord Jesus Christ vouchsafed to suffer for our eternal salvation at those holy places in the last hours of His life."

Any person in a state of grace, devoutly performing the way of the cross, may gain all the indulgences ever granted by Popes to the faithful who visit in person the sacred places in Jerusalem. It is necessary, in order to gain these indulgences, to meditate on the Passion of our Lord; and if the space where the stations are erected, will admit, to go from station to station. But no particular form of prayer is required to gain the indulgences.

The sole conditions to gain these indulgences, according to the best theologians, are two.

1st. To go from one Station to another in regular order. In crowded churches, where this would be impossible for all, it is sufficient for a clergyman with one or two of the laity to make the procession, the people remaining in their places.

2dly. To meditate, to the best of one's ability, on the Passion of our Lord, with some reference at least to the particular event commemorated in each Station.

All other prayers and pious exercises commonly given in books of devotion are most useful to fix the attention, and so help in the required meditation, but they are by no means necessary for gaining the indulgences.

For such persons as cannot visit a church, where the Stations are erected, as sick persons, prisoners, soldiers in camp, sailors at sea, and all others in similar circumstances, there are crucifixes to be had, blessed with the indulgences of the Way of the Cross. All that is required to gain the indulgences from these crucifixes, is to hold them in the hand and to recite twenty times the *Our Father*, the *Hail Mary*, and the *Glory be to the Father*, etc., that is, once for each Station, five times in honor of the Five Wounds of our Lord, and one for the Pope's intentions.

STATION NUMBER ONE.

S TATION number one stands upon the left of the pathway as you commence the ascent of the hill. It faces to the north and is twenty-five feet from the center of the gateway, at an elevation of seven feet and two inches above it and sixty-six feet and seven inches above the foot of the hill, measuring from the lowest point in the meadow to the east. It is backed by trees and a thick shubbery and has a very pleasant location. This station is plainly seen from the highway, and long before you reach the hill. In passing it on your upward journey the direction is west, through a deep excavation and up a steep rise, at the top of which the pathway takes a graceful turn nearly to the south, and leads you on to station number two.

The picture represents Christ, surrounded with soldiers, receiving his sentence. In the background Pilate is seen in the act of washing his hands, significant that he frees himself from the responsibility of the cruel condemnation.

STABAT MATER.

1. Stabat Mater dolorosa,
   Juxta crucem lacrymosa,
   Dum pendebat Filius.

1. Beneath the world's redeeming wood,
   The most afflicted Mother stood,
   Mingling her tears with her Son's blood.

The first station of the "Way of the Cross," on Holy Hill, engraved from a photograph.

JESUS IS CONDEMNED TO DEATH.

Christian Meditations.

Consider how Jesus, after having been scourged and crowned with thorns, was unjustly condemned by Pilate to die on the Cross.

STATION NUMBER TWO.

THE position of station two is on the left of the pathway and facing west. It stands on nearly level ground and is distant from station one, one hundred and ninety-four feet, the longest space between any two stations. Its elevation, above station one, is eleven feet and six inches. It is backed by thick underbrush and some large trees. One, a beautiful hard maple, stands a little too far to the left to be seen in the cut. A few feet north an old bye-road leads around the hill to the east and up to the parsonage in the ravine. This road is well grassed over, shady and free from underbrush. It is a favorite place where many halt to rest and lunch. The direction from here to station three is south by twenty-eight degrees west, and up a gentle rise.

In this picture are represented but four persons. Christ is seen to the front in the act of taking the heavy cross upon his shoulders; while in the background is seen a heartless looking soldier in the act of applying the scourge.

2. Gujus animam gementem,
 Contrisatam, et dolentem,
 Pertransivit gladius.

2. Through her heart His sorrows sharing,
 All His bitter anguish bearing,
 Lo! the piercing sword had passed!

The second station of the "Way of the Cross," on Holy Hill, engraved from a photograph.

JESUS BEARS HIS CROSS.

Christian Meditations.

Consider how Jesus in making this journey with the Cross on His shoulders, thought on us, and offered for us to His Father the death He was about to undergo.

STATION NUMBER THREE.

STATION number three is on the left of the pathway, and is distant from station two, one hundred and five feet. Its elevation above station two is twelve feet and eight inches. The side hill has been graded away about two feet on the back side, to allow the base of the station to stand on a level with the pathway. Here the forest trees begin to show a larger growth. The one seen directly behind the cross at the top of the station is an ironwood of remarkable size, being eleven inches in diameter, Across the pathway to the west is quite an open space, the larger trees for some reason having been cut away. From here to station four the direction is south by thirty degrees west, and the approach is somewhat steeper.

In the picture are seen four persons. In the foreground Jesus is represented as having fallen beneath the weight of the cross, while in the background his merciless tormentors are seen plying the whip of torture.

> 3. O quam tristis et afflicta,
>   Fuit illa benedicta
>   Mater Unigeniti?

> 3. O, how sad and sore distressed
>   Now was she, that Mother Blessed
>   Of the soul-begotten One.

The third station, of the "Way of the Cross," on Holy Hill, engraved from a photograph.

JESUS FALLS THE FIRST TIME.

Christian Meditations.

Consider this first fall of Jesus under His Cross. His flesh was torn by the scourges, His head crowned with thorns, and He had lost a great quantity of blood. He was so weakened He could scarcely walk, and yet He had to carry this great load upon His shoulders. The soldiers struck Him rudely, and thus He fell several times.

STATION NUMBER FOUR.

THE fourth station is the first on the right of the pathway. Its distance from station three is one hundred and thirty-two feet, and its elevation above it is seventeen feet. Its location is on level ground, and in a forest dense and dark. The sunbeams rarely shine on station number four when the trees are clad in their summer's foliage. The large trees seen upon either side are a black oak on the left and a white oak on the right. A sense of deep solitude and loneliness o'ershadows the spot. From this station to number five the way leads, first, to the south and then by a circle gradually again to the southwest.

The picture represents the meeting of Jesus with his mother. The face of Jesus is seen covered with blood. There are five persons represented in the scene, two of whom are women.

4. Quæ mœrebat, et dolebat,
   Pia Mater, dum videbat
   Nati pœnas inclyti.

4. Woe-begone, with heart's prostration.
   Mother meek, the bitter Passion
   Saw she of her glorious Son.

The fourth station, of the "Way of the Cross," on Holy Hill, engraved from a photograph.

JESUS MEETS HIS AFFLICTED MOTHER.

Christian Meditations.

Consider the meeting of the Son and the Mother, which took place on this journey. Their looks became as so many arrows to wound those hearts which loved each other so tenderly.

STATION NUMBER FIVE.

STATION number five stands on the right of the pathway one hundred and twelve feet distant from station four, and at an elevation above it of twelve feet. The hillside had to be graded down four feet to bring the base of the station on a level with the pathway. Across the way, to the east lies the deep valley in which stands the parsonage. From this station, looking upward to the southeast, for the first time since the pilgrimage began, one catches a view of the roof of the church, the steeple and the gilded cross above all. It crops out above the thick forest which covers the hillside and stands in bold relief against the sky. A sharp turn leading nearly to the west soon brings you to station number six.

The picture shows four persons. Jesus is seen bowed down beneath the weight of the cross, while Simon is in the act of helping him to carry the heavy load. Two soldiers in the background are urging them forward, whip in hand.

5. Quis est homo, qui non fleret,
   Matrem Christi si videret
   In tanto supplicio?

5. Who could mark, from tears refraining,
   Christ's dear Mother uncomplaining,
   In so great a sorrow bowed?

The fifth station, of the "Way of the Cross," on Holy Hill, engraved from a photograph.

SIMON HELPS JESUS TO CARRY THE CROSS.

Christian Meditations.

Consider how the Jews, seeing that at each step Jesus was on the point of expiring, and fearing He would die on the way, when they wished Him to die the ignominious death of the Cross, constrained Simon, the Cyrenian, to carry the Cross behind our Lord.

STATION NUMBER SIX.

THE sixth station is on the right of the pathway, situated in an excavation in the hillside eight feet in depth at the rear. Its distance from station five is one hundred and twenty-four feet. Its elevation above station five is only six feet. Upon the surface above the steep embankment the growth of timber is thick and heavy, as will be seen in the picture. Across the path from the station the ground slopes abruptly down to a depth of seventy-five feet. Far down in the deep valley, and almost beneath your feet is seen the roof of the parsonage, while far above you to the southeast is seen the church. The view from station six is one of grandeur and rural beauty. From this station the pathway changes from the southwest to south ten degrees east, to station seven.

The picture at this station represents the meeting of Jesus with Veronica. Jesus laden with the cross is the central object, while Veronica bows in front and offers him a cloth with which to wipe the blood and sweat from his brow.

---

6. Quis non posset contristari,
Christi Matrem contemplari
Dolentem cum Filio ?

6. Who, unmoved, behold her languish
Underneath His cross of anguish
'Mid the fierce, unpitying crowd ?

The sixth station, of the "Way of the Cross," on Holy Hill, engraved from a photograph.

JESUS MEETS VERONICA.

Christian Meditations.

Consider how the holy woman named Veronica, seeing Jesus so ill-used, and His face bathed in sweat and blood, presented Him with a towel, with which He wiped His adorable face, leaving on it the impression of His holy countenance.

STATION NUMBER SEVEN.

THE seventh station is upon the right of the pathway and fronting to the east. It rests in an excavation in the hillside thirty inches in depth. Its distance from station six is one hundred and thirty-two feet. This station is six feet lower than station six, a fortunate circumstance, as it serves to give the wayfarer an opportunity to rest preparatory to the great ascent which is now before him. Two rods to the north a bye-road leads to the west, and by which many visitors to the hill from the south and west travel. Across the way to the east lies the deep valley, where over the climbing grape vines and sumac the beautiful meadows and grain fields are seen far to the east. Heavy timber backs this station and from it the spire of the church is still seen. The direction to station eight is south and up a gentle rise.

In the picture are to be seen four persons. Jesus is represented as having fallen beneath the burden of the cross for the second time. His persecutors are seen standing over Him with scourge upraised.

———

7. Pro peccatis suæ gentis
   Vidit Jesum in tormentis,
   Et flagellis subditum.

7. For His people's sins rejected,
   She her Jesus, unprotected,
   Saw with thorns, with scourges rent.

The seventh station of the "Way of the Cross," on Holy Hill, engraved from a photograph.

JESUS FALLS THE SECOND TIME.

Christian Meditations.

Consider the second fall of Jesus under the Cross; a fall which renews the pain of all the wounds of His head and members.

STATION NUMBER EIGHT.

STATION eight is on the right of pathway, fronting east. Its distance from station seven is one hundred and thirty-eight feet, and its elevation above it is exactly eight feet. The hillside has been graded down five feet to bring the base on a level with the pathway. The trees seen in the rear are poplars. Here the church is again lost sight of, but looking to the east the parsonage is now plainly seen seventy-five feet below you in the valley. Before you reach station nine the pathway leading up from the parsonage is seen upon the left. This was the original path to the top of the hill, though now, owing to the steepness of the route, it is only used by those who have business at the parsonage. The direction to station nine is south thirty degrees east.

The picture in this station contains five figures, three of whom are women. Jesus is represented giving advice and comfort to the women of Jerusalem while the soldiers are seen standing by and looking savagely on.

8. Vidit suum dulcem Natum
   Moriendo desolatum,
   Dum emisit spiritum.

8. Saw her son from judgment taken,
   Her belov'd in death forsaken,
   Till His Spirit forth He sent.

The eighth station, of the "Way of the Cross," on Holy Hill, engraved from a photograph.

JESUS COMFORTS THE WOMEN OF JERUSALEM.

Christian Meditations.

Consider how those women wept with compassion at seeing Jesus in such a pitiable state, streaming with blood, as He walked along. "My children," said He, "weep not for Me, but for your children."

STATION NUMBER NINE.

THE ninth station stands on the left of the path fronting west, in an excavation five feet deep. It is distant from station eight one hundred and forty feet and at an elevation above it of ten feet and four inches. This is a very romatic spot. Just across to the northwest is where the "Shrine by the wayside," and the old station ten formerly stood as will be seen on page seventy-three. Many visitors to the hill drive with their carriages to this point and hitch their teams while they make the balance of the journey on foot. A few feet north the old pathway leads to the east, a shorter cut to the church. From here to station ten the course is directly south and the steep part of the journey begins. This station is backed by a fine cluster of red oaks.

In the picture are seen four persons. Jesus falls for the third time, while Simon is discovered in the act of helping Him to lift the heavy cross. Two soldiers are seen behind, one with an uplifted scourge and the other with a drawn sword.

9. Eja Mater, fons amoris,
   Me sentire vim doloris
   Fac, ut tecum lugeam.

9. Fount of love and holy sorrow,
   Mother, may my spirit borrow
   Somewhat of thy woe profound.

The ninth station, of the "Way of the Cross," on Holy Hill, engraved from a photograph.

JESUS FALLS THE THIRD TIME.

Christian Meditations.

Consider the third fall of Jesus Christ. His weakness was extreme, and the cruelty of His executioners excessive, who tried to hasten His steps when He could scarcely move.

STATION NUMBER TEN.

STATION ten is on the left side of the path and stands in an excavation of eight feet, the top of the ledge being nearly on a level with the station's roof. It is one hundred and seventeen feet from station nine, and has an elevation above it of twenty-two feet and ten inches. Across the pathway to the west the bank descends, from the very edge, and abruptly down to a depth of over one hundred feet. Just opposite this station is a fine cluster of white birch trees on which the initials of a number of names are carved. The larger trees seen in the cut are a black oak at the left and a white oak on the right. From here to station eleven the direction, at first, is to the south and until near it when it circles gracefully around to the southeast.

In the picture are represented four persons. Two soldiers are seen in the act of stripping Jesus of His clothing and drenching Him with water as if to revive Him for the cruel ordeal He is about to undergo.

10. Fac, ut ardeat cor meum
    In amando Christum Deum,
    Ut sibi complaceam.

10. Unto Christ, with pure emotion,
    Raise my contrite heart's devotion,
    Love to read in every wound.

The tenth station of the "Way of the Cross," on Holy Hill, engraved from a photograph.

JESUS STRIPPED AND DRENCHED.

Christian Meditations.

Consider the violence with which the executioners stripped Jesus. His inner garments adhered to His torn flesh, and they dragged them off so roughly that the skin came with them. Compassionate your Saviour thus cruelly treated.

STATION NUMBER ELEVEN.

THE location of station eleven is on the right of
the pathway, and distant from station ten
one hundred and eighty-three feet. It stands in a
slight excavation facing south and at an elevation
above station ten of thirty feet and three inches. This
is the highest elevation between any two stations,
and it is the longest distance between any two,
excepting the first and second. This station is backed
with a very fine grove of second growth of oaks,
poplar and wild cherry. It stands in a commanding
possition and from here the first glimpse of the outly-
ing country is seen far below looking to the southwest. From this station the pathway continues its
circle to a point nearly north-east to station number
twelve.

There are six persons represented in the picture;
but no women. The scene shows a number of soldiers in the act of nailing Jesus to the cross. Jesus is
reclining upon His cross stripped of His clothing and
bleeding from many wounds.

11. Sancta Mater, istud agas,
Crucifixi fige plagas
Cordi meo valide.

11. Those five wounds on Jesus smitten,
Mother! in my heart be written,
Deep as in thine own they be.

The eleventh station of the "Way of the Cross," on Holy Hill, engraved from a photograph.

JESUS IS NAILED TO THE CROSS.

Christian Meditations.

Consider how Jesus, after being thrown on the Cross, extended His hands, and offered to His Eternal Father the sacrifice of His life for our salvation. These barbarians fastened Him with nails, and then, securing the Cross, allowed Him to die with anguish on this infamous gibbet.

STATION NUMBER TWELVE.

APPROACHING station twelve, which is the last
station on the left of pathway, the road
circles again to the south. Its distance from station
eleven is on hundred and forty-four feet and its elevation above it is eighteen feet and two inches. It
stands on level ground, surrounded by a dense
growth of young timber. Directly at the rear are
some fine oaks and poplar, while to the east may be
seen some fine specimens of white birch. The location, is surrounded by deep solitude and gloom, and
one of the most lonely on the whole pilgrimage. Just
west of this station the short cut bye-road enters the
pathway. The direction to station thirteen, after
completing the bend in the pathway, is south twenty
degrees east.

The picture represents the death of Jesus upon
the cross. There are five persons seen, three of whom
are women, weeping beneath and kneeling at the
foot of the cross.

---

12. Tui Nati vulnerati,
    Tam dignati pro me pati,
    Pœnas mecum divide.

12. Thou, my Saviour's cross who bearest,
    Thou, thy Son's rebuke who sharest,
    Let me share them both with thee!

The twelfth station of the "Way of the Cross,"
on Holy Hill, engraved from a photograph.

JESUS DIES ON THE CROSS.

Christian Meditations.

Consider how Jesus, after three hours' agony on
the Cross, consumed with anguish, abandoned Himself to the weight of His body, bowed His head, and
died.

STATION NUMBER THIRTEEN.

WE approach station thirteen where the pathway makes an abrupt turn in a due easterly direction. The station stands on level ground and is on the right of the pathway. It is situated one hundred and fifty feet from station twelve, and its elevation above it is twenty-nine feet and two inches. This station gained, and the church stands out before you in plain sight, looking to the northeast. Across the way the forest is quite thick with small trees, while to the rear and southwest the larger timber has been cut away leaving an open space through which may be seen the beautiful valley far below you. The direction to the last station is east and not far distant.

In the picture the lifeless body of Jesus is being taken down from the cross. Five persons are represented three of whom are women. The countenance of each denotes extreme sorrow and sadness.

13. Fac me tecum pie flere,
    Crucifixo condolere,
    Donec ego vixero.

13. In the Passion of my Maker,
    Be my sinful soul partaker,
    Weep till death, and weep with thee.

The thirteenth station, of the "Way of the Cross," on Holy Hill, engraved from a photograph.

JESUS TAKEN DOWN FROM THE CROSS.

Christian Meditations.

Consider how our Lord, having expired, two of His Disciples, Joseph and Nicodemus, took Him down from the Cross, and placed Him in the arms of His afflicted Mother, who received Him with unutterable tenderness, and pressed Him to her bosom.

STATION NUMBER FOURTEEN.

W E now come to the fourteenth and last "Station of the Cross." It stands upon the right
side of the pathway and is distant from station
thirteen only seventy-five feet, being the shortest
distance between any two stations. It faces to the
north and stands ten feet and two inches above
station thirteen. Some beautiful scrub oaks are seen
in the rear where the ground is free from underbrush
making a very inviting place to rest after the long
and tiresome pilgrimage. The "Bell tower and
Cross," shown on page seventy-nine, is fifty feet east
of you, and the church ninety feet to the northeast,
and up a rise of sixteen feet and six inches to the
stone water table. At station fourteen one is
entranced with the beautiful scene that spreads out
below and around him.

The picture represents the end of the most lamen-
table of all human tragedies, in which six persons are
seen placing Jesus in the sepulcher after the Crucifixion, and three of whom are women.

---

14. Juxta Crucem tecum stare,
    Et me tibi sociare
    In planctu desidero.

14. Mine with Thee be that sad station,
    There to watch the great Salvation
    Wrought upon th' atoning tree.

The fourteenth station of the "Way of the Cross," on Holy Hill, engraved from a photograph.

JESUS IS PLACED IN THE SEPULCHRE.

Christian Meditations.

Consider how the Disciples carried the body of Jesus to bury it, accompanied by His holy Mother, who arranged it in the sepulchre with her own hands. They then closed the tomb, and all withdrew.

15. Virgo virginum præclara,
    Mihi jam non sis amara,
    Fac me tecum plangere.

15. Virgin, thou of virgins fairest,
    May the bitter woe thou bearest
    Make on me impression deep.

16. Fac ut portem Christi mortem,
    Passionis fac consortem
    Et plagas recolere.

16. Thus Christ's dying may I carry,
    With Him in His Passion tarry,
    And His Wounds in memory keep.

17. Fac me plagis vulnerari,
    Fac me Cruce inebriari,
    Et cruore Filii.

17. May His Wounds transfix me wholly,
    May His Cross and Life Blood holy
    Ebriate my heart and mind:

18. Flammis ne urar succensus,
    Per te, Virgo, sim defensus
    In die judicii.

18. Thus inflamed with pure affection,
    In the Virgin's Son protection
    May I at the judgment find.

19. Christe, cum sit hinc exire
    Da per Matrem me venire
    Ad palmam victoriæ.

18. When in death my limbs are failing,
    Let Thy Mother's prayer prevailing
    Lift me, Jesus! to thy throne;

20. Quando corpus morietur,
    Fac ut animæ donetur
    Paradisi gloria.

    Amen.

20. To my parting soul be given
    Entrance through the gate of Heaven,
    There confess me for Thine own.

    Amen.

FROM the fact that the old Stations of the Cross were made from pine, a timber not calculated to long withstand the severe changes of weather in an exposed condition; and as some were getting quite dilapidated and all showing signs of decay, Father Zimmer suggested the propriety of erecting new ones and of a more durable nature. His proposition was favorably received by the Rev. Arch-bishop Heiss, and accordingly, in the summer of 1889, the new Stations of the Cross were begun and completed the the same season.

The contract for building the new stations from brick was let to William Witt of Hartford, for five-hundred and fifty dollars; he to do the work and furnish all materials, which included the zinc crosses and turrets, also the doors and locks, and painting of the wood-work, such as doors and casings. The bricks were made at Granville, near Milwaukee, and were furnished by George N. Hess of Hartford for ten dollars a thousand. Unfortunately they did not prove to be a very good quality. Many of them contained lime pebbles, which were reduced to lime by the burning of the bricks. These slacked by the action of the moisture infused into them by the frosts of the first winter and quite a number burst, defacing the exterior walls. The defects may be seen in the illustrations of stations seven, eight and twelve.

The stations are two feet and four inches wide, four feet and two inches long and seven feet and six inches high to the eaves. They were completed in September, 1889. The receptacles or frames for holding the scriptural representations were made by Peter Westenberger of Hartford for one hundred and forty dollars. They are made from durable wood, as are also the doors which enclose them in the winter season.

The pictures or representations, which were obtained through Hoffman Bros. of Milwaukee, were made in New York city. They are zinc casts, in bass-relief, and are very beautiful illustrations, each figure being wonderfully life-like. The fourteen cost three hundred and fifty-six dollars and fifty-five cents including freight from Milwaukee; making a total cost of the new Stations of the Cross, one thousand and forty-six dollars and fifty-five cents. They form one of the most attractive features of Holy Hill. During the season of divine worship they are always left open for the benefit of all who may visit the place, but they are all closed and securely locked just as soon as the season of solemn service closes. Though the stations are all left open during the season of divine services, the illustrations are well protected by heavy wire screens, and are comparatively secure from the intrusion of the too inquisitive, or molestation by any.

It was quite late in the fall when the stations were completed, consequently they were not dedicated until the following spring. On the twenty-fourth of May, 1890, being the Titular Feast of St. Mary's church on Holy Hill, the new Stations of the Cross were blessed with solemn ceremonies by the Rt. Rev. Mgr. Augustine Zeininger of Milwaukee. The day and the interesting ceremonies, together caused the largest assemblage of people that ever met on Holy Hill previous to that time. It has been estimated that fully four thousand people were present at the hill on that day. Since that time there have been even larger congregations there.

PARSONAGE IN THE GLEN.

Not until the latter part of the month of May does the annual season of divine services begin on Holy Hill; though, at times, pilgrimages are made to the place somewhat earlier. As a rule, however the greater masses, who are accustomed to worship at the hill annually, wait until the time stated arrives. It is at this season that the hill puts on its richest dress of emerald hue; when wild birds, that flit among the overhanging boughs are warbling out their sweetest songs as if to cheer their constant nesting mates; when the wild flowers are blossoming everywhere, and thick beside the pathway, filling the air with a sweet fragrance, as if wafted from some ambrosial censer swung by unseen hands. From amid all these depths of the dark forest's solitude, a sense of solemn, sacred stillness reigns. Then all nature appears, as if adjusting its holy-day attire, preparatory to welcome the countless, penitent throng that soon will come to venerate within this grand and worshipful retreat, the ever Blessed Virgin and adore the Son of God.

TITULAR FEAST: The season of solemn services begins with the Titular Feast of the church on Holy Hill—Mary's Help of Christians—which is always celebrated the twenty-fourth day of May, on account of the many marvelous victories gained by christians at all times over their enemies, contrary to all natural expectations; ascribed to the veneration and the recourse the faithful had to the Blessed Virgin, and particularly when Pope Pius the VII, through his own devotion, as well as through the devotion of all the faithful to the Blessed Virgin was restored to the see at Rome after an exile of five years in France. The same Pontiff declared that a feast in honor of the Blessed Virgin should be annually celebrated on the twenty-fourth day of May, to be known•as "Mary's Help" of Christians; this in commemoration of the aid received through the intercession of God.

THE VISITATION: The feast of the Visitation is annually celebrated on the second day of July. It is well known to all christians that according to Holy Writ, the Blessed Virgin went into the hilly country to visit her cousin Elizabeth. It was on this occasion that Elizabeth, filled with the Holy Ghost, cried out, "Blessed art thou among women, and blessed is the fruit of thy womb—Whence is it, that the mother of my Lord should come to me?" It was on this occasion that Mary said: "My soul doth magnify the Lord, and my spirit hath rejoiced in God my Savior—Henceforth all generations shall call me blessed." Going through the hilly country to Holy Hill the pilgrims are reminded of the pilgrimage made by Mary on that occasion.

FEAST OF THE ASSUMPTION: The fifteenth day of August, which is annually celebrated on Holy Hill, is a day of holy obligation, and is commemorative of the bodily assumption of Mary into Heaven—It is expressive of the joy which the faithful perceive at the consummation of her earthly career, and the crowning reward which God bestowed upon Mary— Elevating her above the angelic choir.

THE NATIVITY: On the eighth day of September the church commemorates on Holy Hill, the happy and joyful day on which the ever Blessed Virgin first saw the light of day; accordingly, the church sings on this day: "Thy nativity, Virgin, Mother of God, hath brought joy to the whole world; for from Thee hath come forth the Sun of Justice, Christ the Lord." The opportunity presented by this celebration on Holy Hill, as a rule gathers an immense congregation from near and far.

HOLY ROSARY: The first Tuesday in the month of October is celebrated on Holy Hill, on account of the "rosary devotion;" a devotion which has been practiced by the regular, as well as the secular clergy, and likewise by the Catholic laity ever since the time of St. Dominic. Leo XIII, the present reigning Pontiff, has time and again exhorted the Catholics to it. The feast of Holy Rosary always comes on the first Sunday in October, but the priests being engaged on that day, and on duty at home, the first Tuesday has been chosen instead.

SPECIAL DAYS: There are also some special days

for divine worship on Holy Hill. As a rule, some day in the month of June is chosen; and most generally it is the "Feast of the Sacred Heart of Jesus," which commonly falls on the first Friday after the Octave of *Corpus Christi.*

In addition to these, there are days chosen by the neighboring congregations for private pilgrimages, which are known and participated in, only by the members af their respective congregations. Such days may vary with every season, though they will never occur on any of the days already mentioned.

The railroad excursions during the summer seasons are becoming quite popular and occur more frequently than in former years. People living in over-crowded cities are glad to avail themselves of these opportunities, and cheap rates of fare offered, to come where they can enjoy a day of rest and recreation, surrounded by the grand and natural scenery such as the forests among the hills afford. Besides the railroad excursions, on almost any pleasant day in summer, there may be seen at the hill large parties of pleasure seekers who come by carriage from all the larger cities for many miles around.

As a brief and accurate description of the church's exterior has already been given, a glance at the interior of this beautiful edifice may not here be uninteresting to the general reader. During his custody of the hill property, Father Zimmer has labored unceasingly from year to year to equip and adorn the church's interior with improvements useful and at the same time durable and ornamental. In his expenditures, for this purpose, he has shown good taste, nor has he been lavish further than the real needs and the means at hand justified.

When he took charge of the church property in 1883 the interior of the church was very scantily furnished, but to-day, in its church equipments, furniture, paintings, statuary and ornamentations, it compares favorably with the best churches in the state.

Whoever visits Holy Hily, at any time other than
on the regular feast days, and would like to take a
look at the interior of the church, he will save
much time and trouble by securing the key before
starting on his journey up the hill.   At all times
when there are no services at the hill the church is
kept securely locked.   The key is kept by Daniel
Goetz, who lives in a little cottage about forty rods
east from the gate to the Hill's enclosure.   No matter if you are a stranger, pilgrim or tourist, the key
will be freely given you, provided, it is demanded in
a civil and gentlemanly way.   Neither Mr. Goetz,
his good wife or any member of his family, from
whom you receive the key, will exact anything from
you, further than a polite request, that on coming
away you will close and lock the door and return
the key to them.   Perhaps, a small fee, for their
trouble, would not be refused, should you feel so
liberally inclined.   But nothing of that kind is ever
demanded by either of them from anyone.

Once in possesion of the key you are ready for
the pilgrimage, which will be found to be a very
pleasant one; though at the same time, before you
reach the summit of the hill, you will become con-
vinced that it is also a very tiresome one.   At first
the rise is slight and gradual, and one sees so many
attractions along the pathway that the ascent is
scarcely noticed until station number nine is reached.
From here to the hill-top the way is so very steep
that it will be necessary to halt many times by the
wayside for rest.   These rests are generally made
before each station, as all love to pass a short time
in viewing the beautiful scriptural representations,

sorrowful and sad though they appear. However, by slow degrees, at length you reach your journey's end, and, as emerging from out the gloom of the darkly shaded pathway you catch the first glimpse of the bright light of day and the beautiful world stretching out so far away, then you will feel well repaid for the time and the toil you have endured.

If this is your first visit to the Hill you will not proceed to enter the church immediately on your arrival. For just before you reach its portals, suddenly you will become entranced by a most magnificent view, spreading out in every direction before your wondering vision. You will love to dwell for a time on the various interesting objects seen far away in the dim distance. And your delight will be increased the more if, happily, you should discern some familiar spot or object, though many miles remote from your place observation.

Having rested from the tedious journey, and being refreshed by the delightful breeze always present on Holy Hill, you are now prepared to take a look at the beautiful interior of the church. This, it is expected, you will do in a manner that is becoming to the sanctity of the place, and not in a careless way, as if to gratify an idle curiosity. The place has been blessed and made holy, and they who have labored to build and furnish it are entitled to your respectful behavior, while they grant you the privileges you are now about to exercise, and which you will no doubt enjoy.

As you enter the doorway, if for the first time, and gaze upon the beauty and harmony of the surroundings, your delight will know no limit, nor can language express it. The light that penetrates the high windows from the many colored glass, gives a rich and mellow luster to each particular object. The beautiful frescoing of the entire interior, will challenge your admiration from the first. Then the tall symmetrical pillars reaching from the floor to the vaulted roof and supporting the interlacing arches will next claim your attention.

Before you advance to examine the beautiful centre and side altars, and other objects of interest, upon either side and at the rear, you will notice at your left, a small shelf on which is placed a register. This is for the use or convenience of visitors, and in which many record the date, their name and residence. If you consult its pages, you will, no doubt, find many names, of persons, with whom you are acquainted. The book contains the names of many who live in distant lands. You will find represented there nearly every state in the Union. You are at liberty to record your own address, but make no further comments than simply the date, your name and place of residence.

A little further, to the right, you will notice a strong iron box securely fastened to the wall. It is placed there for the convenience of those liberally inclined. If you feel disposed to drop a small offering into the opening, you will have done a good act, one which will be appreciated, and appropriated for good uses. You are not asked to give, but the opportunity is there should you feel so disposed.

Still farther to the right is the stairway leading to the gallery for the choir. This is a spacious platform extending across the entire south front. It is

provided with an organ, and is seated with a number
of ordinary low wooden benches. The gallery will
comfortably accommodate about one hundred persons. On nearly all feast days there is present in the
gallery a choir of fine singers which is composed of
musicians from some of the neighboring congregations, most generally from St. Kilian's church of
Hartford. From its high and commanding position
a most magnificent view of nearly the whole interior
of the church may be had from this point.

As you pass down the stairway from the gallery
at the lower landing to the right hand, you will
notice standing in the corner a number of crutches.
These were left by those who had been relieved from
some disease or bodily infirmity through the efficacy
of faith and prayer, and as indisputable evidence of
the miraculous cures which devotees affirmed had
been vouchsafed them through the agency of
Divinity. Some of them were deposited in the little
old log chapel many years ago.

As you view the interior of the church there is
one thing that may strike you as being very odd and
strangely out of place, and especially will this appear so should you view it without any previous
explanation. It is this, that amid all its beautiful
surroundings, the church is seated only with ordinary, low, rude benches. These are arranged in three
rows leaving only two narrow aisles of floor space
extending from the front to near the altar. In all
probability it will never be seated in any other way
for it has been demonstrated on several occasions,
that the church as it now is, will comfortably accommodate fully a quarter more people than if seated

with any of the modern style of pews. Besides, the
floor of the church being so completely filled with
these rude forms presents a peculiarly rustic appearance, and so strangely in contrast with its rich surroundings that the effect is rather pleasing than
otherwise.

The beautiful frescoing of the walls and arched
roof was commenced in November of 1891, but
owing to the severe cold weather was not completed
until the following spring. It was done by the firm
of Liebig and Gaerdner of Milwaukee at a total cost
of one thousand dollars. It is elegant in design
and artistically executed in minutest detail. To
Father Zimmer is due the credit of this beautiful
improvement and decorative finish of the interior of
the church on Holy Hill.

To the right, or east side of the church, and a
short distance back from one of the side altars,
stands the new confessional. It was built by Peter
Westenberger of Hartford at a cost of sixty-seven
dollars. It is commodious in size and conveniently
arranged, and though plain in design is very hand-
somely finished. It was placed in its present position
sometime during the summer of 1891.

To the left of the east side altar you will notice
hanging upon the wall some glass covered show
cases, in which are deposited several pairs of spec-
tacles. These have all been left there by pilgrims who
have visited the hill in times past with impaired eye-
sight, but who, as these mementoes testify, have left
the place with their vision completely restored. There
are also other tokens of remarkable cures which
have been wrought through faith and prayer upon

Holy Hill. These silent witnesses which add their testimony, as is believed, to the direct agency of an omnipotent power, are regarded by all communicants of the church with a due degree of reverence and veneration. In fact, they are looked upon by all who stand in their presence with manifestations of mingled awe and adoration, excepting, it be, by those who are willfully perverse or viciously inclined. The presence of such scoffers here is out of place, and the space they occupy would be more honored by their absence.

There are many other rare and beautiful objects distributed around this retired and sacred domain, things which will invite your close attention and greatly interest you. But there is nothing which you have yet seen that will claim your admiration more than the three magnificent altars located at the rear of the church's interior. These you are at liberty to inspect, though it should be done in a reserved manner, from a respectful distance and in conformity to church etiquette.

NEXT in order to the "Stations of the Cross," the three new and beautiful altars rank as first in importance among the many attractive features which have been added to Holy Hill by Father Zimmer, since he has had charge of the hill property. The new altars were manufactured by Mr. Brielmyer of Milwaukee, in the summer of 1887, at a total cost of eleven hundred dollars. Soon after they were completed they were transported to the hill and placed in position, where, on the fifteenth day of August, 1887, that being the "Feast of the Assumption," they were solemnly blessed in the presence of an immense congregation.

The altars are Gothic in design and construction, and are in beauty and finish specimens of the highest skill of workmanship. The two side altars are about one half less in size than the main or center

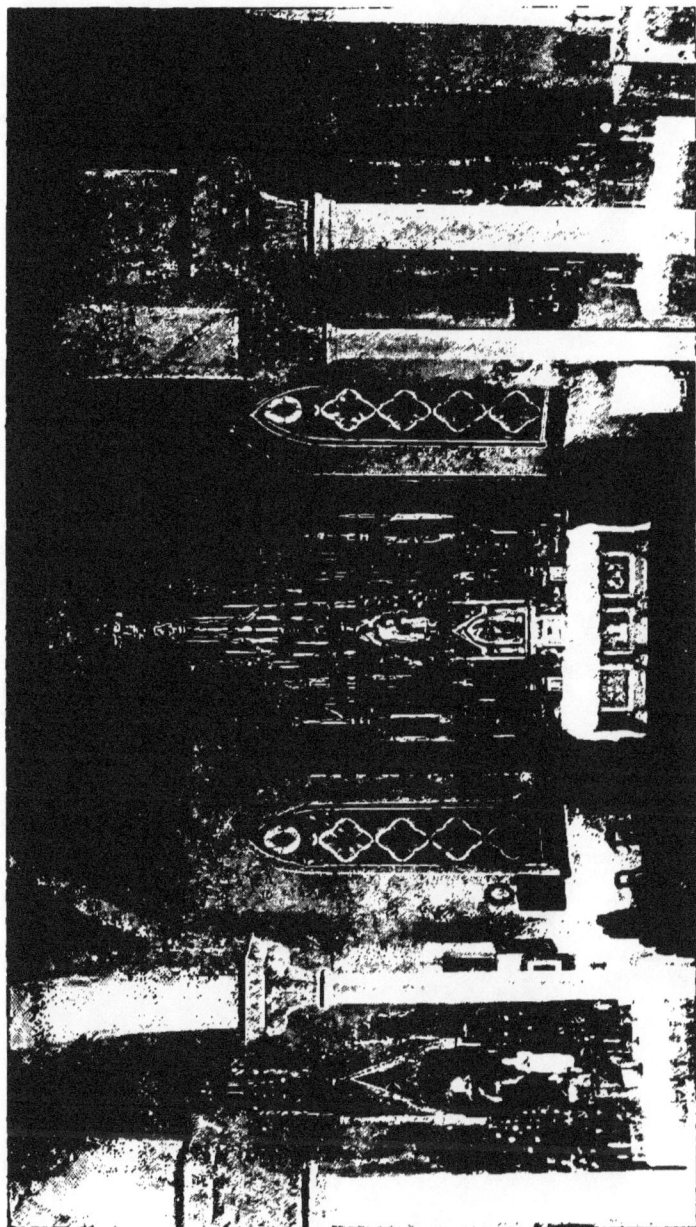

INTERIOR OF ST. MARY'S CHURCH ON HOLY HILL.

altar which is over twenty feet in height. Each of the side altars is an exact duplicate of the other excepting in its furnishings and ornamentations. The right, or the one at the east side of the church, is christened St. Ann, and contains a statue of the saint after whom it is named. The left, or west altar, is christened St. Joseph, and also standing in its center is a statue of that saint.

As the side altars will charm you as being beautiful and pleasing to look upon, so will the main or center altar delight you by its grand and imposing appearance. It is situated well back from the paling to the sanctum, and its retired location makes its appearance all the more majestic. It is dedicated to the Blessed Virgin, Mary Help of Christians. Seen from a short distance this grand altar is beautiful beyond the power of pen to portray. Its lofty spires and minarets, delicate and graceful, loom high up within the dark shadows of the dome. Its gilded cross which surmounts the apex rises high above the architraves until lost among the entablatures of the graceful and bewildering arches.

The center of this altar is ornamented with a large and beautiful statue of the Blessed Virgin and the child Jesus. The statue has quite a history within itself. It was made at Munich, Germany, and was imported to this country in 1876, the centennial year, and was taken to Philadelphia, where it remained on exhibition during the "World's Fair." Its marvelous beauty attracted the attention of many of the visitors and towards the close of the exhibition it was sold to a gentleman from Wisconsin who presented it to Holy Hill. It was first sent

to St. Hubert's church in Richfield where it remained
until the summer of 1878. On the first day of July
in that year the statue was carried by hand by
eighteen young ladies to its destination on Holy Hill.
The distance is nearly seven miles and was traveled
by the young ladies on foot. They were followed by
an immense procession and a number of priests from
St. Boniface, St. Hubert, St. Augustine and other
congregations. The solemn concourse was attended
and guided by a cavalcade of one hundred mounted
young men from the same congregations. The
long journey was enlivened and made pleasant by
prayers and songs which were kept up from the
start to the end of the long journey. Arriving at
the hill, the occasion was celebrated with high mass
and a sermon. The original cost of the statue was
one hundred and fifty dollars, and it was imported
free of duty. It is said that it could not be reproduced for anything like the price which was paid for
it when purchased.

Both the high altar and the sacristy contain
many rare and useful articles of worship, all of which
have been donated by liberal and pious people.
Among these are a monstrance, costing eighty
dollars, which is a transparent receptacle or vessel in
which the consecrated wafer or host is held up to
view before the congregation; a *chiborium*, a safe
or coffer within the high altar, containing the host
or sacred wafers; six elegant Gothic candle-sticks; a
dalmatica, a short outer vestment worn by deacons
at high mass; a surplice, a white garment worn by
the clergy, and three set of albs, an ecclesiastical
vestment of white linen which envelopes the person.

There are also many other articles of minor note, all of which have been donated to the church.

You have now passed a pleasant and interesting hour in viewing the interior of St. Mary's church on Holy Hill. It has been an hour which you will long remember and a visit which you will never regret. If the day has been a pleasant one you will have noticed while there a great number of pilgrims who come and go at almost every hour. Very likely all of them will be strangers to you, and possibly some may have traveled here from their homes hundreds of miles away. You will also have noticed how meekly and quietly each one enters at the doorway, how reverently each deports himself while within the sacred edifice and how sanctimoniously they all depart. These are the real and earnest christians; and though you may not be a member of the church, still if the sentiments of christianity are cherished by you in the slightest degree, you cannot fail to have respect and admiration for those who are so sincere and devout in their ways and manners of worship.

Amonc the many improvements of a lesser nature contributed to Holy Hill through the personal exertions of Father Zimmer during his custodianship of the property, the first, worthy of note, is the bell-tower illustrated on page 79. Sometime previous to 1885 a fund was raised by contribution to purchase a bell for the church on Holy Hill. The bell was purchased of the manufacturers, McShane & Co., of Baltimore, Maryland, and cost, with the mountings, two hundred and seventy-five dollars. On its arrival at the hill in the summer of 1885, owing to its great weight, it was deemed unsafe to hang it in the belfry of the church, and after some deliberation it was decided to build a separate belfry or tower for that especial purpose. Accordingly the contract to build a suitable tower for the bell was let to Henry Dietzler of Hartford at an expense of two hundred and fourteen dollars.

The tower is substantially built, being fourteen feet square at the base and tapering slightly from the ground upwards. The lower room, about fourteen feet high, is shingled and has but one opening, a large door on the north side. Above this is the bell-room proper, each side being open lattice work for the sound waves to pass freely out in all directions. Above the bell-room a six sided spire extends upwards, which is surmounted by a large wooden cross, the extreme height being thirty-five feet from the ground. The lower room is used as a store house and contains the old wood stations.

The bell tower is located forty-five feet south and west from the church and about the same distance east from station fourteen. It is one of the interesting features of the hill and from its elevated position the great bell sends forth its tones reverberating through the valleys among the hills for miles around. The tower was completed and the bell hung in the fall of 1885, at a total cost of nearly five hundred dollars. The bell alone weighs twelve hundred pounds and cost eighteen cents a pound at the factory.

About six feet to the west of the bell tower stands the ancient cross, erected by Romanus Goetz in 1858. It is the oldest land mark and sacred relic on Holy Hill. Though it has withstood the fierce storms of more than one-quarter of a century, and its exterior shows plainly the ravages of time, still it stands proudly erect and continues to stretch out its friendly arms above the heads of the tens of thousands who yearly congregate within the presence of its fostering care and sacred influence.

Across its arms, and deeply carved in Roman charac-
ters, is the German inscription, still legible as when
engraved by Mr. Goetz thirty-five years ago—"*Ich
bin das Leben, wer an mich glaubt wird selig.*"
Owing to want of space this seems to be an abbrevia-
tion of the English translation of the scriptural
text which reads—John, 11th Chapt, 25th and 26th
verses—"Jesus said unto her, (Martha) I am the
resurrection and the life: he that believeth in me,
though he were dead, yet shall he live; and whoso-
ever liveth and believeth in me shall never die."

One of the best improvements for the accommodation of the traveling public, and especially for
those who visit Holy Hill from long distances and
by team, was instituted by Father Zimmer during
the summer of 1890. Until then to reach the hill
from the highway was over a private driveway a
distance of eighty rods. This privilege was accorded
to all for several years by the owner of the land, Mr.
Mathias Werner, as an accommodation merely. But
as the road was simply private property, no road
work was ever done upon it, and in consequence, it
was most generally in a very poor condition for
travel. Seeing the great need of better facilities for
reaching the hill from the highway, Father Zimmer,
sometime in September of 1890, purchased from Mr.
Werner, for the church, a strip of land one and one-
half rods wide and seventy-five rods long, leading
from the highway to the gate at the northeast
corner of the hill property. The price paid for this
narrow roadway was one hundred dollars, quite a
sum for three quarters of an acre of land in this
mountainous country.

It was so late in the season when the land was purchased that there was no work done towards putting it in order for travel until the following spring. Then the contract was let for clearing it from stones and rubbish and grading it down to a proper level. The contract for doing the work was awarded to Daniel Goetz for forty dollars; and it was a very large amount of labor and a most excellent piece of work which he did for that small amount of money. But in addition to the money he received for his labor, he already has, and should continue to receive, the grateful thanks of all visitors to the hill for years to come.

One of the most serious inconveniences that visitors to the hill have had to contend with in past years is the lack of suitable accommodations for man and beasts while there. Coming from any principal point one may, the journey is long and the road to be traveled is indeed rough and very hilly. So much so, that when one reaches his destination, both himself and his team are weary, thirsty and hungry, and there is but little chance to satisfy either. Of course, on ordinary occasions, when the hill is not thronged with visitors, there are places where those who happen there then can have these wants supplied and at very reasonable prices.

Now, as in former years, Mathias Werner keeps a hotel, if such it may be called, near and in full view of the hill. It is only a short distance east from the entrance to the bye-road leading to the church property. A cut of Mr. Werner's hotel is shown on page thirty-four, and as will be seen, it is quite a goodly sized cottage. The front is built from

brick, while the rear part is constructed from hewn
logs. It has a very decided rural appearance, inas-
much as architecture was not considered in its
construction; yet it is all the more home-like and
inviting by reason of its simplicity and rustic
appearance.

The hotel can accommodate as many as twenty
guests at meals, but not more than half that number
with comfortable lodging. The fare is simple, but
at the same time abundant and substantial, and
the charges are extremely moderate. Mr. Werner's
accommodations are ample for all ordinary days,
but on feast days, excursions and other like occasions his resources are inadequate to entertain even
one in every hundred that craves his hospitality.

Mr. Werner is a very genial host, and strives to
entertain his guests, especially if they are strangers.
There is no end to the fund of information of which
he is possessed and which he is ever ready and
delights to impart to others regarding the place.
His long residence among the hills has given him a
thorough knowledge of all the incidents and interesting features connected with Holy Hill. Strangers
who visit the place will find his cottage a pleasant
home, and Mr. Werner, as interesting and as useful
as a guide book.

Within the last few years, or since the parsonage
has been untenanted, on nearly all days of a general
gathering, meals are served at the priest's house in
the glen by Mrs. Daniel Goetz. A good dinner may
be had there for twenty-five cents, provided one is
fortunate in getting a place at the table. This, however, you are by no means certain of, the applicants

COTTAGE HOME OF DANIEL GOETZ.

for such privileges being always greatly in excess of the accommodations at hand. Sometimes Mrs. Goetz serves meals at her home to strangers, tourists or pilgrims when visiting the hill, though she can entertain only a small number at a time owing to her limited means of accommodation.

The accompanying engraving illustrates very accurately the pleasant cottage home of Daniel Goetz. It is situated about one hundred rods northeast from the parsonage in the glen, and from this point, looking in that direction, is seen standing out plainly in view. The log house and other farm buildings adjoining it are situated in the depths of a very fertile valley. The place has a somewhat secluded, but a rather inviting look, and all its surroundings are suggestive of the real home comforts of an unpretentious life.

The photograph after which the cut was made was taken about the middle of July 1891. The young lady, Miss Katie Goetz, had just brought out the dinner to the faithful watch dog, whose kennel was underneath the granary, and the dog was about half way out when the plate in the camera was exposed to the light and all before it. The instrument stood near the pile of planks by the garden fence. The picture shows the large apple tree in the garden in its fullest summer foliage, but it does not show its fruit, with which it was well laden at the time. The picket fence completely surrounds the large fruit and flower garden just in front of the house. Mrs. Goetz is quite a florist and during any of the summer months the garden contains a great variety of beautiful and fragrant flowers.

The home of Daniel Goetz is indeed a lovely spot, and its surroundings are picturesque in the highest degree. It was from this point and just southwest of his cottage that the view of Holy Hill was taken after which the large and beautiful engraving, as shown on page thirteen, was made. From here, not only the entire north and east sides of the hill are plainly seen, but also the church on the hill-top and the parsonage in the deep ravine among the hills. From here, looking directly west, Station one and the wicker gateway to the hill are plainly seen. As resting here, on any of the feast days, you can see the entire, vast and countless procession as it passes and repasses through the open gateway to and from divine worship in the church on the hill's summit. To him who loves quietude the home of Mr. Goetz will be found well adapted to his wants and comforts while sojourning at the hill.

As the two places already described are the only ones where entertainment may be had by those who visit at the hill, and as both of these are limited in their means, and often inadequate to supply the demand, it will follow, that excursions, picnics and family parties should go prepared; and particularly is this so, should they visit the place at any time during the pleasant summer days. On such occasions a well filled lunch basket will not come amiss, and will contribute greatly to the comfort and pleasure of the time. Also a sufficient quantity of feed for the team should constitute a part of the outfit, and none, who can conveniently provide such, should neglect this, at times, very important sustenance. There is one thing more; all should take the precaution to water their team at some convenient place before reaching the hill, as quite frequently the wells in the vicinity become exhausted by the constant drain which is made upon them in the early part of the day, and frequently by noon there is but little water to be obtained, even for man, and much less, and very often none, for his tired horses.

It is now, however, an assured fact, that before the end of the present season ample accommodations will be provided for entertaining all who may visit Holy Hill, even on the days of general gatherings, at least in the way of a substantial meal. On the authority of Father Zimmer, it is stated that plans are being perfected to erect a mammoth dining hall of suitable dimensions to feed the immense throng that congregates there on any of the noted days of worship. It is said that this needed accommodation for visitors was inaugurated at the instance of some Milwaukee gentlemen, philanthropic men, who evidently have noticed its great need, and who have liberally donated to the good work.

As now contemplated, the new dining hall will be located in the pleasant valley just east from the parsonage and convenient to the only well on the grounds. When completed the new improvement will be under the supervision and management of Mrs. Daniel Goetz which is a sufficient guarantee that all who apply will be amply provided for.

As this chapter will practically finish the descriptive part of Holy Hill, the writer cannot let the opportunity pass without paying some tributes of respect to the hardy band of old settlers who first

invaded the forests among these hills. The home of
Daniel Goetz illustrates very fairly the kind of tene-
ments that were in use by all of the early settlers;
but the picture in itself, does not convey much of
an idea of the condition of things as they once existed there. For though the fields now look fair and
pleasing to the eye, being free from the heavy forests
that once encumbered them, yet it took years of toil
and hard labor, by that sturdy band of old pioneers,
to remove these and subjugate the land to a condition fit for agricultural purposes.

As may be seen in the picture, the buildings are
all of the simplest kind, made in the most primitive
style of architecture. Nearly all were constructed
from such materials as were conveniently at hand,
and most generally cut or dug from land ajoining.
In addition to the unskilled labor, it required but a
small outlay of money for lumber, hardware and
glass to construct these humble log abodes. They
were not spacious nor elegant, but they supplied all
the needs of a comfortable home for these hardy
dwellers who settled among the hills. These log
cabins must be quite durable for after having been
used for nearly fifty years most of them are still
occupied, and until quite recently no other kind of
habitations was met with for miles around.

The early settlers of this locality were most
assuredly a class of men who were possessed of
real manly courage, as, from the first, there was
nothing especially inviting nor encouraging for them
to build homes among these rugged hills. They also
must have been men who were endowed with good
physical strength and indurance to withstand

the many hardships necessary to remove the heavy forests and convert the rough land into such fruitful farms as may be found here on every hand to-day.

There are quite a number of the original pioneers still living, and who are now in the enjoyment of their hard earned possessions; but, alas, very many of them have passed life's boundary line and have retired from the scenes of their earthly labor forever.

"For them no more the blazing hearth shall burn,
  Nor busy housewife ply her evening care;
No children run to lisp their sire's return,
  Or climb his knees the envied kiss to share.

"Oft did the harvest to their sickle yield;
  Their furrow oft the stubborn glebe has broke;
How jocund did they drive their team afield!
  How bowed the woods beneath their sturdy stroke!

But they performed their mission well, and when departing left to posterity a good inheritance and their honored names—Names and deeds that the living of to-day and future generations should long cherish in grateful remembrance and forever perpetuate in story, history and song.

Many years ago it was the province of the writer to frequently visit these early settlers in their humble log cabin homes. At such times he had ample opportunity to note well their contented and simple modes of life, and it is with feelings of gratitude and thankfulness that he now makes due acknowledgement for the many courtesies extended to him by these commonplace, yet hospitable, old settlers. No honor which the living can bestow is too great for the services which they rendered; and all the praise that posterity can offer would come far short of being adequate compensation for the years of hardships and privations which they underwent.

On the twenty-second day of February, 1888, the writer, by request, composed and read a poem before the Old Settlers' Club of Washington County, at West Bend. Though the poem was intended to commemorate the old settlers in general, yet it contains many passages that very fittingly apply to the early settlers in and around Holy Hill. For this reason, and also, that the poem has remained unpublished, excepting in pamphlet form, the author deems that it may be interesting and not improper to introduce it here.

THE OLD SETTLERS.

The early settlers—who were they?
Looking around us here to-day,
We see, amid this gathering here,
The form of many a pioneer.
Easy to single them out here now—
Privation and toil stamped on each brow;
Bowed by hardship, age and decay,
Bearing their locks of iron-grey,
Only the relics of toil and care,
Only a remnant of those that were,
Only a handfull, aged and grey,
Are left to meet with us here to-day.

Yet these are the men who first trod on this soil,
And these are the matrons who shared in their toil;
Yes, these the Old Settlers who early and first,
Like an avalanche on-to a wilderness burst.

Yes they are the ones who left kindred mid tears,
Who quitted the scenes of their earlier years,
  With hearts full of hope for their future success;
  Who labored for years amid want and distress,
  In the depths of a desolate, dark wilderness,

Whose solitude only was broken and stirred
When the shriek and shout of the savage were heard.
Such then was the prospect your vision first caught,
Ere your stalwart arms such changes had wrought.

When you entered the forest no highway was laid,
Yet you wielded the axe 'till a pathway was made.
Now struggling mid thickets, or fording the stream;
The progress was slow, and the faithful ox team

Was swayed by the gad with a "haw" and a "gee,"
As you followed the trail by the "blaze" on the tree;
'Till at last, weary worn, the cumbersome load
Reached the spot you had chose for the future abode.

A moment you rested and the prospect surveyed;
If a task was before you, you were not dismayed.
You had come there to stay; the forest must yield,
And bow to the axe you stood ready to wield;

And the wondering savage through fear stood aloof,
As you ate the first meal with the sky for a roof.
Then soon from the depths of that forest arose
The echoing sound of the strong sturdy blows.

'Twas the music of progress that plays in the van,
And which heralds the coming of civilized man.
'Twas the sound of an axe, with stroke upon stroke,
As you sought with a will for the heart of the oak;

You found what you sought, but no poet can tell
The joy that was yours when the first giant fell,
For its ominous sound smote the savage with fear,
And he knew that his time of departure was near.

. Ere long in the midst of that forest appeared
The log cabin home in the patch you had cleared;
Rude in its structure, in compass 'twas small,
But it served for a home and gave shelter to all.

Of the straight forest trees were its walls out and in,
Betwixt which the chinks were secured with a pin
Or wedge made of wood, and to keep out the air,
Each crack was mud plastered and pointed with care

The floor of split puncheons, laid in a rough way,
To a level was adzed on the first rainy day.
One window for light, and one only—no more,
Had its place by the side of the log cabin door,

That turned on wood hinges with hoarseness and din;
Its latch was a lock—when the string was pulled in.
Thus the humble log cabin secure from the blast,
With its shake shingled roof was completed at last—

And the family moved in, and we're free to declare,
That amid all the wealth of proud palaces rare,
Was less happiness found, or less genuine bliss,
Than you "old settlers" knew in a cabin like this.

Through the long winter evenings the pioneer sire,
By the light of a "slut," or the bright blazing fire,
Sat astride of his bench, while enjoying a smoke,
And would fashion a helve, or an-ox bow or yoke,

Just above him on hooks, there rested in quiet,
The time honored musket, and powder horn nigh it;
The same his great grandsire, once handled with will
'Gainst the foes to his country on old Bunker hill.

And in many a conflict, great service had done—
Heirloom of his sires! how he prized that old gun!
And he fashioned away, with thoughts on the wing,
Of years that were past, or the future might bring,

While the young mother sang her sweet lullaby o'er
Her babe which she rocked on the rough cabin floor,
As she patched at the wamus, or darned up the sock,
Until the short hand pointed ten by the clock.

And your pioneer's life was free from all guile;
You dwelt in contentment, you cared not for style;
Was happy though clad in the backwoodman's dress
Your wants were but few, and your resources less.

To the stranger the cabin door never was barred,
Though rations were scant, the last loaf was shared;
And with you hospitality was not a mere name,
For the latch string was out, no matter who came.

Yet 'twere tedious to tell, far too lengthy to trace,
Each step from a cabin to your proud dwelling place.
Of your hardships and toil, your dangers and fears,
Shall our hist'ry record of your earlier years—

What your labor has bought, what posterity gains,
One glance at creation around us explains.—
A country as fair and more fruitful by odds,
Than any yet known on this footstool of God's.

Yet the prospect so fair which around us expands,
Is the price of hard labor produced by your hands,
And the fruits of abundance enjoyed by us now,
Were begotten by toil and the sweat of your brow.

Changed are the scenes, from those you first knew;
The forests are gone, and the land where they grew,
Expands in broad fields, both fruitful and fair,
For the hand of industry still guards them with care,

And the ox teams of yore are but things of the past;
Now you ride in a carriage and more stately its cast,
And no longer you dwell in the log cabin rude,
For a mansion now stands where a log cabin stood,

And the voice of the savage, who dared to dispute.
Your right to possession is silent and mute.
The sound of the waters that flowed from the hill,
Is hushed by the hum of the wheel in the mill.

And below in the valley, across the ravine,
The iron bridge spans where you forded the stream.
So the infant who slept to its mother's sweet lay,
In the zenith of manhood now greets here to-day.

All is changed—and time with its cycling years,
Is fast thinning the ranks of the "old pioneers,"
Though death still pursues while the latest survives,
Yet God in his bounty hath lengthened your lives;

He hath spared you to live, to partake and enjoy
Of this feast as the fruits of your early employ—
Allowed us to meet you, your children and theirs,
To thank you, and honor your fast fleeting years—

To bless, ere you've taken your final sojourn
To the old settlers' home whence no travelers return.
Yet still as the years pass successive away,
May we meet you again, as we meet you to-day.

Yes meet you as now, and in friendship still clasp,
Each "old settlers" hand in fraternity's clasp,
And when thou art gone, may posterity's tears,
Long moisten the graves of the Old Pioneers.

MIRACULOUS CURES.

THE steadfast belief and sincere devotions, as manifested by the communicants of the Catholic church, in conformity to the tenets of their creed, are only equaled by their earnest zeal and faithful following of their religious teachings. Among no other religious denominations are these true christian qualities so plainly marked, and so characteristically exemplified, as we find them here; for certainly, by no other religious sect have doctrines and forms of worship remained from the beginning so sacredly unaltered.

One of the most wonderful attributes ascribed to Holy Hill, as claimed by many, and especially by the Catholics, is that some unseen and omnipotent power pervades this sacred domain. A mysterious energy, with an efficacy so benign, that can, and does in a miraculous way cure various forms of human afflictions. By the faithful followers of Christ it is believed that this unseen power is made manifest in a transcendent way through a divine agency; and that it comes to the afflicted penitent who through confiding faith and fervent supplications, devoutly invokes divine aid; that it is derived through the mediation of the Saints, and here particularly, through the intercession of Mary, Mother of God, they believe God to be moved to grant their requests. It is a beautiful christian faith.

The cases cited, and vouched for as having been cured, are numerous, and as to the nature of the diseases, they are multiform. Regarding the authenticity of many very remarkable cures reported, not only are there records in proof, but also there are living witnesses who will testify to the genuineness of the cures as cited. Many of those who bear witness to these wonderful and mysterious cures are now living in the vicinity of Holy Hill. A number of them are well and personally known to the writer, and they are persons of the highest respectability; those whose truth and veracity were never yet questioned by any. They are persons who, having personal knowledge of the facts, are so firm in their belief of these cures that their faith cannot be shaken by any arguments than can be produced against them to the contrary. Besides, we have the testimony of those who have themselves been cured, many of whom are now living in the enjoyment of good health, in addition to which, and as accumulative evidence, there are now preserved in the church a number of crutches and other tokens of disease which have been deposited there by those who have sought and found relief from various diseases.

Yet notwithstanding all this evidence so authentic, being so sacredly preserved and so conveniently at hand, there are those who not only discredit the statements made by others in regard to the verity of these cures, but who do not hesitate to scoff and ridicule others for enjoying their honest convictions: for enjoying a belief that is founded upon scriptural teachings and sound theological investigation; a belief which does not in the least molest or interfere with the rights or happiness of them or others.

These scoffers are generally of that class who pretend to disbelieve in everything that has for its support laws governed by nature or divinity; yet who, by a close intimacy, would reveal to you, that they are converts to some dogma that is founded upon mere fallacy alone. Such individuals are common and are to be met with among all nations of the earth. They have existed through all ages from the beginning of time. Nor are they confined to the ignorant alone, but you may discover them among men of science, professors and statesmen, many of whom have been known to have been slaves to the fascinations of strange and unnatural beliefs. Fallacy, like prejudice, is impervions to logic, and no argument addressed to the reason has any effect upon its power or prevalence.

The *Scientific American* in a recent number, speaking of this subject asks—"Why is thirteen an unlucky number? What possible connection has the assemblage of thirteen persons at a dinner with the death of any one of them during the ensuing year?

If fourteen dine together, there is certainly a greater chance that one of them would pass away within the twelvemonth than if one less sat at the table, and yet this is not the common estimate. There is not a housekeeper in this city (New York) who would seat thirteen at her table without a feeling of regret, and the great majority would not entertain a company composed of that number for any consideration whatever."

"There are scores of absurd beliefs connected with the moon and its phases. The effect of its "changes" on the weather is a matter of almost universal belief, although nearly all of our renowned scientists have agreed that there is not the slightest observable dependence between them. There is probably not a person in the whole country who would not, if he had his choice, prefer to catch the first glimpse of the new moon over his right shoulder while large numbers are rendered quite miserable, if they happen to see the narrow crescent on its first appearance, over their left shoulder."

"The prevalent belief that Friday is an unlucky day regulates in many respects the business of the world. Those who are ready to assert that they have no feeling whatever on the subject are very careful when starting in any new enterprise, or in choosing the date for an entertainment or a marriage, not to run counter to this popular fallacy. Some years ago an English ship owner, finding none of his ships would go to sea on Friday, owing to the feeling among the sailors, determined to cure their madness if he could. He therefore laid the keel of a vessel on Friday, made every contract for its con-

struction on Friday, and launched the craft on the
unlucky day. He christened the ship Friday and
found an old sea captain by the name of Friday
whom he made master for her first voyage. After
great difficulty in securing a crew she sailed on a
given Friday for her destination. She was never
spoken after the pilot left her. It is strange how
one such incident will deepen a prejudice already
existing in the minds of many. The presumption is
that when the ship encountered her first storm, the
sailors, who are proverbially superstitious, became
apprehensive and took to the boats, leaving the
ill-fated craft to founder in midocean and perished
themselves in like manner.

The paper cites a number of other cases showing
to what an extent the minds of even intelligent
men may become prejudiced in favor of such abnor-
mal beliefs, beliefs that cannot be sustained by any
logic founded upon science, and incompatible with
the laws of nature or even common sense. But never-
theless such individuals are found among all nationalities and in every station of life; those who will
cling tenaciously to some delusive fantasy, while
they ignore the truths of divinity and reject the
teachings of the righteous.

In the succeeding chapter is given the history of
a number of well authenticated cures. The writer has
selected only those which are the more prominent,
and such as are susceptible of the best proof. As to a
few of the cures related, the author has a personal
knowledge of the facts. It must not be inferred,
however, that the cases related are all the cures that
have been consummated on Holy Hill. There have

been many other cases reported, but which are of minor consequence. It is also well known that a number of cures have been effected there, where the few who were knowing to the facts, have been enjoined to the strictest secrecy by those who were cured or benefitted. And this, for the reason, that the convalescents chose to avoid the annoyance of frequent and public interviews in relation thereto; and for the further reason, they did not want to suffer the ridicule with which the evil disposed and wickedly inclined might assail them.

It is also true that not all who seek relief there meet with the desired reward for all they ask. None but the truly meek, devout and purely penitent may hope for those blessings which none but the ever Blessed Virgin can bestow.

ONE of the first cures reported as having taken place at Holy Hill was brought to the personal knowledge of the writer while boarding at a hotel kept by Carl Klose at Schleisingerville in the fall of 1858. At that time a peddler was stopping at the hotel who carried his right arm in a sling. He was selling religious pictures and a few other light goods which he carried in a box suspended from his shoulder by a wide strap. He would start out in the morning and sell his wares among the farmers and return in the evening. At times he would be be absent for two or three days. He gave his name as Anton Meister, said he was a mason by trade and had worked several years in Chicago; that about a year previous he was stricken with paralysis, the effects of which had left his right arm powerless. He could not work at his trade and had taken up peddling to earn a living. One evening he returned to the hotel quite late and appeared to be greatly delighted about something. Soon he began to explain to those present that he had, that day, suddenly recovered the use of his right arm. When questioned as to the facts, he answered—"I was peddling to-day in the neighborhood of a big hill some eight miles south of here. I eat my dinner with an Irish family near the foot of the hill, and before leaving I spoke of the big hill so near by, when the man informed me that about four months before they had raised and blessed a cross on the top. As I am a Catholic I traveled up the hill to spend a time in prayer. On coming to the cross I knelt down and prayed, and in that prayer, as I had often done before, I asked and begged to be relieved of my affliction. When I arose I took my purse from my pocket and opened it, as usual, with my left hand, and without being aware of what I did, took a coin with my right hand and dropped it in the box that was fastened to the cross. Then, for the first time I was aware of what I had done, and in my joy I exclaimed aloud—"My God, is this possible!"—Then to assure myself that it was really so, I swung my right arm around and over my head. It was all right again, and I had not used it for over a year. I was so overjoyed that I spent the rest of the afternoon in prayer on the hill, and left there only two hours ago. I did not stop to peddle anymore, and only called at a little grocery near St. Augustine's to pay for my breakfast and last night's lodging." The sincerity with which he related his experience caused none, who heard him, to doubt it. The next morning he sold his peddler's outfit to the landlord for a small amount and left rejoicing on the first train for Chicago.

The case of Louis Marmes is the second cure reported at the hill, and is one of the most authentic and wonderful in the whole catalogue. It is authentic because Mr. Marmes lived in the vicinity at the time and he is still living to-day, as also are many others who were knowing to the circumstances and who will testify to the truth of this statement. It is wonderful because from a helpless invalid he was restored to complete health in an incredibly short space of time. Mr. Marmes was keeping a small store at the time near St. Augustine's church, one and a half miles east of the hill. He was terribly afflicted with rheumatism and suffered intense pain. He tried every known remedy, consulted physicians, but all to no purpose, nothing contributed to his relief and he continued to grow steadily worse. His limbs became powerless and his form wasted to a mere skeleton. One day someone chanced to relate in his presence about the wonderful cure of Mr. Meister at the hill. This seemed to inspire him with a new hope and he then determined, as a last resort, to undertake the pilgrimage to the hill. Soon after, on a bright morning in June, supported by his two crutches and an attendant upon either side, he started for the hill on foot. It took them four hours to make the journey and reach the hill-top. Mr. Marmes, being a devout Catholic, prayed constantly while on his journey up and down the hill. It was

night when they reached their home, but Marmes
remarked that he felt better than he had for months.
He returned to the hill the next day but took only
one attendant with him. The third day he returned
alone, sustained only by the aid of his crutches.
Late in the afternoon of that day some people at
Mr. Werner's heard someone shouting and singing
near the gate-way to the hill. Looking in that direction they saw Marmes coming on one crutch and
waving the other in the air above his head. When
he came near to them he suddenly halted, waved
his crutch above him and shouted—"I am cured—
My pain has left me and blessed be Mary for ever."
The fourth day he left one crutch on the hill, and the
other on the fifth day, using only a cane. On the
seventh day, being completely restored, he left his
cane. His crutches have been preserved in the church
where they may now be seen. Mr. Marmes rapidly
gained in strength and is now a robust man. Some
years later he came to Hartford and started a store,
and at the same time he kept a store in Woodland
and another at Kaukauna. A few years ago he
closed out his business here and went to Antigo
where he now resides. He was known far and near
as "Cheap John," and it pleased him greatly to be
thus addressed.

A very remarkable cure is reported by Mr.
Werner who keeps the hotel, and which, he says, he
can vouch for as being in every particular true, for
as he added, "I saw it with my own eyes." He says:
—"In the summer of 1862 there came to my hotel a

STAIRWAY OF CHURCH ON HOLY HILL.

mother with her five year old daughter. The child was helpless, and her mother said she had no use of her lower limbs and had never walked a step in her life. I assisted the lady to take the child up the hill to the old log chapel. When we went in she seated the child on a bench and then addressed herself to prayer. There were two other ladies on the opposite side near the altar engaged in devotion. All at once the child sprang off the bench, walked across the floor and picked up a handkerchief which one of the strange ladies had accidentally dropped. The mother, on seeing this, was so delighted that her joy knew no bounds. She picked the child up, kissed her many times and wept over her for joy. She then prayed for a time giving thanks to the blessed Virgin Mary. When she had finished her devotions we started on our return down the hill, the child walking all the way back to the hotel. They stayed with me a few days and then returned to their home. If I heard their names at the time I have forgotten them now, and also their residence which I now think was in Fond du Lac county; but all the other circumstances were true as I have related them."

In the month of August 1881, there came to the hill a stranger who made his home with Mr. Werner for quite a time. He was a man about seventy years old who said that he was an Englishman and kept a hotel at La Salle, Illinois. He said that for many years he had been terribly afflicted with the headache, and from which he was suffering greatly at the time. He had tried all the remedies that had been recommended and had changed his residence several times but was unable to obtain the least relief. He could not endure the sun's rays and was obliged to keep in the shade during the heat of the day. In going to the hill he would take the cool of the morning and remain in the shade of the woods until late in the afternoon. On the sixth or seventh day, while praying at one of the stations, all at once he felt a strange sensation in his head and instantly the pain had left him. He remained at the hill a number of days afterwards, and to assure himself that he was permanently cured, would go up the hill in the hot sun with his head bare. He was quite bald and the sun burned his head so the whole top was one blister, but there was no return of his headache. Some years later he wrote to a friend, whose acquaintance he had made while there, saying that he had never had the least pain in his head since leaving the place. When he came to the hill he was a church member and a Protestant, but after his experience there he espoused the Catholic religion.

The case of John Merkel, who was cured of a very malignant cancer, one of the worst type, is so well substantiated by living witnesses that no question was ever raised as to its reality; even in the minds of the most skeptical. Mr. Merkel is now living with his family just one mile east from Holy Hill. For several years previous to 1884 he was terribly afflicted with cancer of the face. He submitted to skilful medical treatment by eminent physicians, and tried many remedies recommended by nonprofessionals. Though many remedies had power to afford some transient relief from pain, yet none could cure or check the ravages of the dire disease. Portions of his cheek, lip and nose were eaten away, and finally one eye became involved and the loss of sight was threatened. At this stage of the disease he was told by his physicians that he was incurable; and the only thing that could be done, to alleviate his sufferings, would be for him to submit to the knife. As he was an old man and with a constitution greatly impaired, he chose rather to die than to undergo further torture. Accordingly he made every preparation for death. He disposed of all his worldly effects by will, and commended his spiritual welfare through the mediation of a priest to God. At this time he was living directly west from the hill, and by his door many pilgrims passed almost daily on their journey to and from the place of worship. Noticing this, and believing that he had but a short time to live, one day he made a solemn vow that he would go once each day to the hill and there repeat a certain prayer. Soon after he had commenced to execute his promised task he became aware that his pain had entirely left him. Then an examination of the tumor proved that the decayed portions of the flesh were dropping off and the wound showed evidence of healing. From that time he gradually grew in health and strength, and eventually the ulcer completely healed. The writer was personally acquainted with him at the time the disease was in its worst stages, and has met him often since. The cure is perfect, only the scars remaining to add their testimony. Though now over eighty years of age Mr. Merkel still enjoys good health. He cultivates forty acres of land and works some at his trade, that of a stone mason.

A daughter of Herman Verhalen, residing at Franklin, Milwaukee county, was cured of insanity by the fervent prayers of her father. Her case had been pronounced as incurable by her attending physicians, and her father was himself nearly crazed over the unfortunate condition of his child. He had heard of the many wonderful cures that had been wrought on Holy Hill through the intercession of the saints. Therefore he resolved to make a pilgrimage to the hill on behalf of his daughter, she not being in a condition to undertake the journey in person. He went and remained there three days, praying fervently each day from station to station. On the fourth day he returned to his home, and was delighted beyond measure to find his daughter in her right mind, perfectly cured. She is now a highly educated young lady and at present is engaged in teaching school. Though a number of years have passed since the cure was effected, the lady has never experienced the least symptom of her former malady.

Two cases are reported which were of a similar character, the patients being middle aged women, and both residing in Milwaukee county. Their respective postoffice address is—Mrs. John Woelfl, and Mrs. John Brums, of St. Martin's, Wis. Both were nearly helpless invalids when taken to the hill, being completely prostrated by nervous debility. They remained at the hill for several days, making the "Stations of the Cross" each day and praying devoutly at every station. At the end of six days each confessed that she was completely cured. They stayed there several days later to regain their strength, and on leaving for their homes said they had not felt so well in many years. Neither of them has ever been sick since her experience at Holy Hill.

The case of Mr. A. Sherrer of New Munster, Wis., is cited as a very miraculous cure and is given in detail as follows: On the 25th day of August 1887, Mr. Sherrer was out with his gun shooting squirrels. As he discharged his gun, a muzzle-loader, from some cause unknown, the breech-pin flew out and backward followed by the burning charge. His right eye, being open, was completely filled with the grains of powder causing him intense pain. He was carefully treated by the local physician for two weeks following the accident but was unable to obtain the least relief. The doctor, seeing that he was growing worse instead of better, sent him to a celebrated occulist in Milwaukee for treatment. There he submitted to an operation for the removal of the grains of powder from his eye. He continued in the doctor's care for three months, during which time he suffered the most excruciating pain excepting when under the influence of opiates. In July of the succeeding year he again returned to Milwaukee and placed himself under the treatment of one who was skilled in eye surgery. He remained there until the latter part of August with no abatement of the terrible pain which he endured. At length, on the advise of others, he abandoned all medical treatment and made a pilgrimage to Holy Hill. He arrived at Mr. Werner's on the 24th day of August 1888. His stay at the hill was for only about ten days, and his experience while there is given in his own words, and is as follows: "The first day that I went up the hill, though I prayed long and earnestly I was unable to sense any alleviation of my pain; but on the second day, while praying in the chapel before the altar, and in the presence of others, every particle of pain suddenly vanished. It had been just one year since the accident happened, and during that year I had suffered untold agony and, to be so instantly relieved of all pain whatever, caused a thrill of joy to take possession of me, such as I cannot describe, nor can I ever forget it. It is over a year since I had that pleasant experience on Holy Hill, yet I never had the least pain in my eye afterwards, and can now see and bear the light as well as ever I could."

Perhaps, one of the most remarkable cures ever effected at Holy Hill, was that of Miss Ida Klingel of Burlington, Wis. This lady had suffered greatly for a number of years with sore eyes. Her eyes and the lids were badly inflamed and her vision became so impaired that she could scarcely distinguish large objects, even at short distances. She could not bear the light of day and suffered constant pain. In this condition, at the age of twenty-one years, she took counsel with Dr. Schneider, an eminent occulist of Milwaukee. She was too poor to undergo the treatment which he recommended, and in her trouble a friend advised her to hold a nine days' devotion on Holy Hill. She immediately made preparations to make the pilgrimage, and in June 1887 made her first appearance at the hill. When she came there her eyes were securely bandaged, and to further protect them from the light, she wore a broad visor projecting from her brow. She was assisted up and down the hill for eight days in succession, and though she prayed fervently at every station, she did not seem to receive the slightest benefit. On the ninth day, accompanied by her assistant, she repaired early to the hill, praying earnestly and long at each station. On her arrival at the chapel, before the altar, she implored divine aid through the intercession of the Blessed Virgin. On her return, and when she appeared before the last station, which is station one on the upward journey, she suddenly exclaimed—"My God, I can see!" and so it really was. She took the bandage from her eyes; gazed long and silently upon the statuary illustration in the station and wept aloud. She then turned to view the pleasant fields, the green trees and beautiful wild flowers around her. It was a sight that had not blessed her vision for years, and she stood like one entranced, her joy being too great to find expression in words. She remained at the hill two or three weeks later, and improved in health so rapidly that before she left she could read newspapers of the finest print. It has been four years since her happy experience at Holy Hill, and she has never had any return of the disease. She is now married, healthy, prosperous and happy.

No case which has yet been cited is more susceptible of proof than that which relates to the cure of Miss Clara Kroeger of Milwaukee. This young lady had been afflicted with a peculiar disease of the eyes known as ophthalmia. The disease had existed for a number of years and had become firmly seated. Her father, being a man of means, the junior member of "Kroeger Brothers," Grove street, Milwaukee, had procured for her the services of the most eminent occulists in the city. Though she had been skilfully treated for over two years, not the slightest improvement could be perceived in her condition, but instead she continued to grow worse. At last she was nearly blind and suffered much pain. Her father had heard of the many wonderful cures that had been perfected on Holy Hill, and he persuaded his daughter, who was then twelve years old, to accompany him there in the hopes of obtaining relief. On a bright day in June 1886, the father with his little daughter arrived at the hill. In the morning of the first day on which they ascended the hill, artificial means were resorted to, in order to open her eye-lids. Together they took the pathway of the stations of the Cross, each reverently praying by the way-side as they climbed the steep hill. The daughter having implicit confidence in her father, was inspired to believe that relief from her troubles was near at hand, and earnestly she prayed for that deliverance to come. When they reached the chapel their vows and promises were renewed amid their united supplications for relief, and which was there granted unto them. She was completely cured and they returned to their home the next day, the daughter being to all appearances as well as ever. She immediately resumed her studies and is now an estimable and highly educated young lady. Since their experience at the hill, the father and daughter continue to make a pilgrimage once each year to the sacred place where the young lady received such gracious benefit.

A young son of John Mundschau, now residing at Dousman, Waukesha Co., was cured of epileptic fits, by persistent prayer in 1887. He was subject to them for many years and the spasms were growing, both in frequency and intensity. After his visit to the hill he was never troubled with them again. He is now a young man and physically strong.

There is one more cure that should have mention, and that, because of its recent occurrence. It is the case of Miss Katie Galinski of 676 Fifth Avenue, Milwaukee. The cure took place on Holy Hill on the second day of July, 1890. Soon after, an account of the cure was published in the Milwaukee *Evening Star*, and from that paper was copied into a number of newspapers throughout the state. Mr. Galinski is a Pole, but his wife is German and they talk German at their home. Being interviewed by a reporter soon after the occurrence, Mrs. Galinski made the following statement which is given here in her own words: "My little Katie here, who was six years old on the twenty-first of February last," said the mother, looking down upon a bright little girl clinging to her dress, "is the one who was cured of a terrible disease. In the month of August last year, sores began to appear upon the little one's face and body. Finally her whole head became one entire sore, so that her hair had to be cut off short. In October we took her to Dr. E———— who told me the child had scrofula and that it would take a long time to cure her. He gave me a prescription to be filled which he said would give her relief. I got the medicine which cost fifty-five cents and it lasted just one week. For a number of weeks I continued to have the medicine put up and gave it according to directions. At times it seemed to help a little, but I could see no real good effects from it. This continued through the winter, and the last of May I went to the doctor again and asked him if he could not do something to help my poor child. He looked at her head, said it was a bad case, and there was danger of it getting worse as the weather grew warmer. He then gave me some salve to apply to her head, and to my great joy the sore disappeared after a few applications. But in a few days the disease broke out on one of her knees, and it soon looked as if the limb would have to be taken off to save her life. On the first day of July, when I was completely filled with grief and despair, I noticed my neighbor in the yard hurrying about as if preparing for some unusual event. I asked her if she was going away, and she answered that she had arranged to go to Holy Hill the next day. 'Oh, that's the place where people go to get cured, is it not?' I remarked, 'Yes.' She replied 'Well then, I think I will go, and take my Katie along.' In the evening I asked my husband's permission to go and he readily consented. I secured a ticket at once, and the next day found us at the famous hill. When we alighted from the 'bus Katie was in great pain and said, 'I can never walk up that steep hill.' I told her she must try and we finally reached the top. Then I told her she must pray to Holy Mary. 'Mother I can't pray, I am in such pain,' replied Katie. 'Well, but you must ask the Blessed Mary to pray for you.' We walked about, went into the church, drank of water, prayed and when dinner time came we walked down the hill. Katie said no more about her pain, and I forgot to ask her about it. After dinner we walked up and down the hill again and she got along nicely and did not complain. On our way home we were caught in a thunder shower and Katie got very wet. I was afraid she might take cold and as soon as we got home I put her into dry clothes and placed her in bed. I usually had to get up two or three times every night to tend her, but that night she slept soundly. Next morning about nine o'clock, while sewing, I heard a sudden "bump" up stairs, and the next moment Katie was by my side. 'Did you fall out of bed?' I asked—'No mamma I jumped out,' she said. 'Well but let me see your knee,' I asked. To my great surprise the sore was gone, and in its place only a few red spots

were left to mark the place where it had been. For
nine days we prayed and gave thanks together, and
now Katie is as well as ever. One thing is certain—
I shall always be thankful that I took that journey
to Holy Hill."

Many other cases might be cited in proof of this
mysterious and wonderful power to eliminate
various diseases from the human body. But the
addition of more would not convince those who are
so prejudiced in their minds, that they will not stop
to listen to any arguments however reasonable they
may appear. It was this same perverse will and
stubbornness of disposition that caused the Jews to
disbelieve in the teachings of and discredit the miracles wrought by Christ. Simply because they did not
want to believe, they would not believe even those
things which they saw with their own eyes.

From the cures already mentioned, it will be
perceived that there is a peculiar sameness extending through all the cases cited. In no single instance
was there a cure effected, or relief obtained, except
through the prayerful supplication of the afflicted
one, or the prayers of others in his behalf. It will also
be seen, that the experience of all, at the moment of
relief, was in each case nearly similar, neither having
had any warning or previous admonition of what
was about to take place. And further, among all
the cures cited, is there no single instance where the
convalescent had a return of his former complaint.
Therefore, it must be inferred that the same restor-
ing power or element that brought relief in any one

instance, was manifestly the curative agency present in every case.

There are some who are too skeptical to admit that these cures emanate from a divine influence, but who are willing to concede that they actually did take place as stated. Such persons usually have some theory which they ascribe as the real cause; and most generally they claim that the cures are brought about by a sudden change in air, water and diet; or that they are produced by a radical change in the scenery and surroundings of the patient; such as the immediate transfer from a bustling city life to haunts of the loneliest solitude. As to this, it has been shown that in every case that has been reported, the cure was consummated in a far too brief space of time for such a theory to be even admissible. And again, how can such a theory be made to apply to the daughter of Herman Verhalen?

It is not within the province of the writer to elucidate or more fully explain the beneficent power by which these cures are said to be effected. As to the incentive cause, and the subsequent mysterious manifestation tending the produce the desired and ultimate result, he leaves it for those who are better versed in theology and the scriptural teachings to more fully interpret.

If, as is maintained by many, these cures are perfected from causes other than at divine instance, then there is wanting some authentic proof, based upon scientific reasonings, to substantiate such theories. In the absence of such proof, as is now the existing status, it is much better, more charitable, christian like and pleasant for all concerned, to let those who do believe enjoy their honest convictions. Those who believe, in all sincerity, that these cures in every instance are wrought directly through divine influence, when sought with abiding faith and earnest prayer, are entitled to that privilege, and ought not to be subject to molestation or ridicule from any; especially as it interferes with no man's rights, private or public, and is, to them, a sacred enjoyment, secondary to none which earth affords.

In concluding this chapter the author wishes to add, that none of the cases quoted has been colored in the least from the original statements of those cured, or by some one in their behalf who was well knowing to the facts. On the contrary he has thought proper to modify the statements of a few somewhat, though the main features of each coincide with the facts as given. The statements in the case of John Merkel are certified to by his wife Elisabeth, which certificate, among others, is now on file in the archives of St. Mary's church on Holy Hill. That the incredulous might have access to a personal statement by the cured, the writer, as far as practicable, has been particular to give correct names, nature of each disease, the date of cure and the present postoffice address of such as are now known.

THE HERMIT OF HOLY HILL.

W AS it not for the fact that the history of Holy Hill would appear incomplete without the story of the wonderful "hermit" being told, this and the subsequent chapter would have remained un-written but from the fact that so strange and eccentric a personage, was once and for many years domiciled among the lonely hills, a mention of his presence there and a short sketch of his life is deemed to be a pertinent part of the hill's history. He was a man whose uncouth habits, strange ways and odd methods of living were so at variance with those of mankind in general that his name and fame soon became familiar to all for miles around. In fact, his presence lent such an influence to the place that, for a time, the very name of the hill was changed. Hermit Hill was the name commonly applied to the

place during his sojourn there, and it is even known
and called by that name by many of the older people
to-day.

The date of his advent among the hills is somewhat shrouded in mystery and is very uncertain, as
not all of his contemporaries agree as to the exact
time. It is, however, generally conceded that he
must have come sometime in the spring of 1864. He
may have been there for some time before his presence
was discovered, as he studiously avoided all contact
with the outside world, and maintained while there
a life of profound seclusion.

His presence on the hill was first noticed by the
late James Gorry, at least he was the first to make
mention of the fact. His farm was just a half mile
due east from the hill, and, as he related, while seeding in the month of April in the year referred to, he
saw one morning what appeared to be a man on the
summit of the hill. He took but little notice of the
object as it was customary to see people on the hill
at all hours of the day. The next morning he saw
the form again, and clearly outlined against the blue
sky. It appeared to be that of a man, near the cross
and in the attitude of prayer. This continued for
several mornings in succession, and until his seeding
was done, when, in company with his neighbor,
Murtha Doon, he went to the hill to investigate and
see who the "lone pilgrim" might be.

After toiling up the hill, and on their arrival at
the top, they found themselves in the presence of a
stranger. As he was in the act of praying they kept
at a distance until he had finished his devotion.
They then approached and addressed him in a

friendly manner, asking several questions. Their
interrogatories were met by a haughty stare and a
forbidding frown from the stranger. His replies
were short and evasive, and were anything but
interesting or satisfactory to his would-be interviewers. The little he said was in broken English
excepting once he replied in German, yet neither
language appeared to be his mother tongue.

He was above the average height of man and was
apparently quite well advanced in years. His form
was spare, but stately and commanding. His large
dark eyes looked piercingly out from beneath the
heavy black eye-brows which set off with good effect
his ample and intellectual fore-head. A heavy
mantle enveloped his form and hid from sight his
nether garments, while his head was covered with a
black slouch hat. In one hand he carried a long,
heavy, rude staff and in the other an open book.
From his looks and manners it did not require the
wisdom of an expert to determine that the man was
laboring under some aberration of the mind. This
much discovered Mr. Gorry and his companion,
which caused them to withdraw from a further
investigation.

On their return home they had a wonderful story
to relate of the strange person they had met on the
hill. The news that a hermit had taken up his abode
on Holy Hill soon spread over the near neighborhood and he had many interviewers each day. A
party going for that purpose one day discovered
that he had made his home in a sort of a "dugout"
in the lower part of the deep ravine, opposite to
where the parsonage now stands. It was a rude

affair and served only as a lodging place, the front being protected by old logs and bark, such as he could conveniently scrape together. There were few articles to be seen and no utensils for cooking, yet he must have made it serve as a sort of a lodging place for some time.

Soon visitors and curiosity seekers began to flock to the hill, all anxious to catch a glimpse of the now noted man. Seeing so many every day seemed to make a change in his behavior for the better. He was more talkative and pleasant in his ways and actions, and finally ventured out for a call on his nearest neighbors. They assisted him by giving him food and other needed comforts of life. Finally a few neighbors clubbed together and assisted in building him a rude log hut. It was very diminutive in size and of the rudest construction. A picture of this humble hermitage may be seen on the opposite page. The cut shows indistinctly for the reason that it was made after a small photograph. This photograph was taken in 1872, by the late F. C. Kendall, and is the only one of the hermitage now in existence.

The old hermitage was located on the south slope of the ravine and stood about five rods east from the northeast corner of the parsonage. It fronted to the south and the little shed to the east of the main part was covered with bark. It contained only one door and a small window, which were on the front side, and above the door was nailed a rude cross. The whole surroundings were then of intense loneliness, and the majority of those who found themselves in the presence of this lonely haunt

THE OLD HERMITAGE.

hurried by with mingled feelings of awe and fear.

As the hermit grew on friendly terms with a few of his nearer neighbors, he gave to them his name, which he said was Francois Soubris; but further than this, he could not be induced to tell anything of his past life. That, to him and all others, was as a sealed book. From his conversation, it developed that he was of French origin, for when he chanced to find one who could talk that language, it seemed to have the magic effect of unloosing his tongue, and he would talk to such for hours together.

His aversion to strangers was great and undisguised, and he shunned their company as best he might. If he could not escape from interviewers and they plied him with too many questions, their inquiries were sure to be met with an answer in the nature of a rebuke for their impertinence. He also entertained a great dislike for women and children, and in this instance the dislike was mutual, for had he been a ghost of the dead, they would not have exercised more caution to avoid a personal encounter.

To all who took notice of his strange actions, random speech and bewildered gaze, it was plainly evident that he was a kind of monomaniac; one in whom some single faculty of the mind had become deranged and subverted from its rational functions. At times he would have lucid intervals when his mind would appear clear and his conversation would not only be interesting, but would indicate an intelligence of the highest order. Such spells of sanity were often abruptly terminated, and as suddenly would his mind lapse into a state of semi-oblivion to all things present.

By some it has been erroneously stated that he came to the hill with the object of being cured of some bodily ailment, and that he was cured of rheumatism or some other lameness. All such statements are wholly without foundation. His disease was purely of the mind, and not of the body. No one who ever interviewed him was mistaken as to his true malady. All his speech and actions plainly showed that was laboring under some great burden of mind. He had a few old books which showed unmistakable evidence of constant use. When left alone, he kept up a constant, incoherent conversation with himself, and would at times while in the presence of others. A poetical description of the hermit is given by the author in his poem of the "Hermit of Holy Hill," which was partially published in 1881, shortly after the hermit departed. It is thought proper to introduce it here.

THE HERMIT OF HOLY HILL.

He made his advent here, among
The hills, when all was wild and young:
When dwellers few and far between,
Had chanced this wild romantic scene.
He came, yet no one knew from where,
But they saw and felt his presence there.

At morn, upon the summit high,
His form was seen against the sky,
And bowed, as though in earnest prayer,
With head uncovered, bald and bare.
His long thin locks of silvery grey,
Each passing breeze did sport and sway;

While ever and anon he raised
His face aloft and heavenward gazed,
And held his long lank arms on high,
As though he sought to reach the sky.
And thus for hours he knelt there low.
Unconscious of the world below.

At mid-day oft his form was seen
Far downward in the deep ravine—
It was his home, where years he strayed
Alone, beneath the wildwood's shade;
And many oft have met him there—
An aged man, tall, thin and spare.

His form erect, and shapely wrought
As statue, carved with studied thought;
Of lofty mien and step that showed
He once had trod some courtly road;
While in his bearing lingered yet
The cast which princely sires beget.

His ample brow and head denoted
  The many years of study spent,
When he to science was devoted
  In youth's bright days that came and went.
That came and went, but left their trace,
For time or toil can ne'er efface,
Or blot from off the face that lives,
That dignity which learning gives.

His large dark eyes, whose piercing look,
  The firey blood of youth could quell,
And send them shiv'ring from that nook,
  Betrayed his wand'ring mind too well,
And showed a burdened soul o'erwrought
With hardship, trouble, care and thought.

Clad in a robe of modest sample,
  And black as any coffin's pall;
With flowing sleeves, and collar ample,
  Its spacious folds enveloped all.

'Twas gathered tight about the middle,
And fastened with a silken girdle,
Whose tasseled tips securely tied,
Hung pendent from his dexter side.

A Maltese cross of burnished gold,
Beneath his mantel's outer fold,
Reclined upon his breast, dependent,
By chain of beads with pearls resplendent,
Within one hand a book was shielded;
An oaken staff the other wielded.

A misanthrope who hated men,
But long the monarch of the glen;
Who held mankind in fear and awe,
More rigid than the written law;
Who did o'er them a power exert,
A charm that none might dare avert;
But all obeyed the iron will
Of him, the Hermit of the Hill.

The history of the hermit will be but briefly related in this work, for to follow in detail all the important passages in the life of this strange adventurer would require volumes. Owing to limited space only the main features of his life can be given here. All the events of the hermit's life have already been written by the author poetically, but they are too highly colored with romance for a work of this kind, and only a few of the more commonplace sketches of the work have been introduced. The information from which this chapter is written is derived from one who confessed that it was communicated to him by the hermit shortly before his departure from the hill.

From the best information, Francois Soubris was born about the year 1804, near the city of Metz, in Lorraine, then a province of France. He was the

only child of Louis Soubris, who was at that time
an officer in the French army. When young Soubris
was only eight years of age his mother died,
and as his father was shifting about from place to
place with a detachment of the French army, he was
sent to Mannheim on the Rhine to live with an uncle,
his mother's brother.

He was quite a prepossessing child, and his uncle
soon adopted him as one of his own family. He
sent him to school where he advanced in his studies
rapidly, and was always at the head of his class.
When he was sixteen his uncle sent him to a
university at Frankfort-on-the Main, and where he
completed his education, graduating at the age of
nineteen years.

On his return home he assisted his uncle in his
business. Their home was just outside the city of
Mannheim where his uncle owned and cultivated a
large vineyard, the fruit of which was converted into
wine. Besides being a producer, his uncle did a
large business in buying and exporting wine. For
convenience in shipping he kept a large wine ware-
house in the city near to the river Rhine. Here
Francois spent the greater part of his time, looking
to the shipments, keeping the books and attending
to the correspondence.

He had been in his uncle's employ about two
years when a circumstance arose which changed his
whole subsequent course of life. In the vicinity of
his uncle's home, and on the usual route to the
business part of the city, was a hotel, or *Wirths-
haus*, kept by a middle aged man whom his customers called Caspar. His place was a favorite resort

for business men, being outside of the bustle and
turmoil of the city, and here the uncle of Francois
spent much of his time, especially evenings. On his
way home from the office the young man was
accustomed to call there for his uncle and wait to
accompany him home.

Old Caspar had but one child, a daughter
Margaret, who at the time was fifteen years of
age. She had a lively disposition and was a very
handsome and attractive young lady. It was her
custom, at times when many guests were present,
to assist her father in waiting upon them. Sometimes when Francois called in the evening for his
uncle he would order a goblet of wine, which
Maggie would bring and place before him. During
her leisure moments she would seat herself at the
table opposite to him and they would converse
together in low tones, sometimes for hours. A
warm attachment sprang up between the two which
soon developed into ardent love, the result of which
proved to be a life of misery and sorrow for both.

Old Caspar and the young man's uncle soon took
notice of their growing attachment and after a brief
consultation concluded that it must be terminated
at once. They were of different religious castes,
which their elders deemed was a sufficient barrier to a
closer union. The young man was forbidden the
house or further interviews with the young lady, and
she was guarded with the utmost vigilance and kept
from his presence.

Francois, foiled of his dearest object in life, medi-
tated revenge on both his persecutors, and was not
long in maturing his plans. He had one real friend

and companion in the son of a ship captain who transported their wine from Mannheim to the sea-board. He was about his own age and to him he confided all his plans, which his friend promised to assist him in carrying out. By his aid a private meeting between the two was arranged to take place the next evening at the house of a friend. That evening Francois did not return to the home of his uncle nor did he ever again. That was to be his last evening in Mannheim and he was patiently waiting for the hour, set for his farewell meeting with Maggie, to come. Both were promptly on hand at the appointed hour; an hour, to them, of mingled joy and sadness; an hour in which hope and faith constituted the sustaining elements in the hearts of each. Francois disclosed to her that every-thing was in readiness for his departure for America that very evening, and promised that as soon as circumstances would permit he would either return for her or send her the means to follow him. To all which Maggie readily consented, and with many assurances that each would remain constant to the other, though it should take ten years to consummate their plans and ardent wishes, with a fond farewell they parted, not to meet again in many years.

Francois was soon upon the street where he found his friend waiting. In less than an hour they were on board the old captain's barge, drifting rapidly downward with the swift current of the turbulent waters of the river Rhine. On their arrival at the sea port the old man and his son soon found the master of a sailing vessel who agreed to give Francois transportation across the ocean for his help on shipboard. As the ship was to sail the next morning he was secretly conveyed aboard the same evening. The next morning at break of day the ship weighed anchor and stood out to sea.

Francois helped the sailors to unfurl the great sails one by one until all her canvass was spead to the wind. Then he felt relieved, proud and defiant, as he felt the staunch ship bounding over the waves and saw the shores of his native land fast receding from his view. It was this feeling that caused him in after years to recall the circumstance with the following sad refrain:

> "Ah! Maggie dear, you never knew
>   The high resolve that filled my brain,
> As on the deck I stood, while flew
>   Our bark like sea-bird o'er the main—
>
> As one by one the sails unfurled,
>   I thought it was a manly part,
> To go and battle with the world,
>   And make me worthy of thy heart.
>
> My days have been many and sad since then,
> Yet no love of my heart has ever been
>   Like the love I bore for thee.
> I have won honor and fortune and fame,
> But what now to me is an empty name,
>   Since thou art lost to me?

Before leaving it was arranged that all correspondence between the two should be conducted through and intrusted to their mutual friend.

The ship was destined for Quebec, where after a stormy voyage of many weeks it safely landed, and Francois set out to look for work. Being a stranger in a strange land he was unable to procure anything excepting odd jobs and poor pay. He struggled on for over two years and then left for New York City. Here he met with no better success, and after another year spent in a fruitless search for profitable employment he left for Baltimore and thence for Charleston. He was unused to hard manual labor and his knowledge of the English language was too limited to secure for him a position such as his education would otherwise warrant.

He had been in Charleston only a few weeks when, to his great delight, he chanced to meet one evening a gentleman who had been a student with him at Frankfort-on-the-Main. An intimacy sprang up at once between him and his new found friend, who was engaged in teaching a private school, giving lessons in the French and German languages. It so happened that his friend had, a few days previous to their meeting, been appointed to a clerkship in one of the government departments at Washington, and he therefore prevailed upon Francois to take charge of his school which he consented to do. His friend assisted him for two weeks, when seeing that he filled the requirements admirably, he turned it over to his full charge. It was a position that he was well qualified for and he held it successfully for nearly five years, relinquishing it then of his own choice.

He was now, for the first time since he landed in this country, earning good wages, and at the end of the first year he proceeded to carry out his agreement with Maggie by sending her the money to pay her passage to this country. During the four years he had been absent, he had sent her many letters and had always received prompt and assuring answers. But to the letter containing the money he received no reply, though he waited patiently for over a year and wrote many letters of inquiry. One day he was surprised to receive a letter mailed from Mannheim, which on being opened was found to contain the identical money he had sent over a year before but in it not one single word of explanation. He was greatly worried over the mysterious affair which he was unable to solve. He wrote a number of letters afterwards but no answer ever came back to him, and as the years passed by, time but increased his strong desire to go and investigate that, which had deprived him of every pleasure in life.

He had now acquired considerable means and he decided to resign his position and return to his native land. Accordingly, in August, 1833, he closed up his affairs and took passage for his early home. He reached Mannheim the latter part of September after an absence of nearly ten years. He arrived in the city quite late in the evening and proceeded directly to the hotel of old Caspar. Upon the streets he did not recognize any one he ever knew, and certainly none would have known him. Ten years at that period in life had wrought quite a change in his appearance.

As he entered the hotel door he noticed from the first glance that everything there had undergone a great change. Old Caspar was no longer in his accustomed place, but a much younger man instead. The old customers who were wont to be seated around the tables were there no more, but strangers filled their seats. He took his place at the table and called for a glass of wine. While sipping away, he kept close watch of the door through which, in years gone by, he had seen Maggie so often enter the room, but she came not. He waited patiently until the customers had gone to their homes, then he ordered more wine and invited the landlord to drink along. He took a seat at the table and the conversation began. He asked in regard to old Caspar, and was informed by the young man that he had died some six years before. Then he enquired as to his uncle, and was answered that he was still living, though confined to his house a helpless invalid. Gradually Francois shifted his conversation until he ventured to enquire what had become of old Caspar's wife and his daughter Maggie. The landlord being warmed with wine and interested in the stranger, proceeded to give an account of the family, but he little thought that his recital fell like burning coals upon the brain of his stranger guest.

His narration of the facts ran as follows: Said he, "soon after old Caspar died, the widow and her daughter, being without much means, were forced to give up this place, and they moved to a little cottage about three blocks from here where they are now living. About a year after her father died, the young lady married a boatman on the Rhine. He proved to be a reckless, drinking sort of a fellow, and on his return up the river, about one year ago, at Coblenz, he and two of his companions were drowned by the upsetting of a yawl boat. Those knowing to the facts say that the accident was the result of a protracted spree. Since then the old lady and her daughter, who has one son, have been living at the place I mentioned, and are now in quite reduced circumstances."

The landlord had hardly ceased speaking when Francois asked with great haste and anxiety the name of Maggie's husband. As he had already surmised, from the beginning of his entertainer's story, it was none other than his *trusted friend.* He understood it all now and his heart was steeled against any developments that might follow. He said to his informer that he had known the family in former years and that he greatly desired to see them once more, and asked him if he would kindly lead the way to the cottage where they were living. To this request the landlord readily consented, and the two were soon wending their way in that direction. When they drew near the humble cottage his guide pointed it out saying: "There it is, I will now leave you by yourself."

A light was still burning and its cheerful rays shone through the half curtained window. As Francois passed through the little gate he paused an instant to scan the interior of the room, and saw within, the old lady seated in a chair rocking a child, but he was unable to discover any other inmate. He could bear the suspense no longer and, stepping quietly up to the door, rapped. His summons was answered by the old lady who appeared at the door with the child in her arms, and though she did not recognize him, she bade him enter and be seated. He informed her that his errand was to see and speak with her daughter for a few moments. She answered that Maggie was not feeling well, but stepped to a door leading to another room and called her. In a

few moments Maggie appeared through the door,
but, Oh! how changed in those ten years since last
they met! Her pale cheeks and emaciated form
showed too plainly that she also had undergone her
full share of sorrow and disappointment. They
gazed intently at each other but only an instant, and
then each others names simultaneously fell from their
lips—Francois! Maggie! Then followed an interval of
ominous silence.

All the sorrow occasioned by their final meeting
will never be known. Suffice it to say, that Maggie
was the first to break that silence, and told, amid her
tears of anguish, how his friend continued to visit
her for years and exchange the letters that passed
between them. How he came one evening with a
letter which purported to be written by a doctor
from Charleston, America, and which stated that
Francois had died and was buried there; in proof of
which she produced the forged and deceitful letter.
Then she spoke of how, after her father's death, his
friend continued his visits to her, and finally confessed his love and offered his hand in marriage.
How she at first and for a long time refused to
accept his offer, until at last in consideration of his
professed friendship for him, together with the
pecuniary circumstances of herself and aged mother,
she had yielded, though reluctantly, to his proposal,
and that she had never known one moment of happiness since then.

When Francois left the little cottage that night
it was with a lighter purse and a heavier heart than
when he entered it. His remorse for the ingratitude
he had shown his uncle: his ignominy for the base

treachery of his trusted and confidential friend and
his lost confidence in mankind, all had conspired to
crush his heart and threatened to destroy his reason.
When he again crossed the threshold of that home,
now forever dead to him, the fresh air of the September morning came like a cooling balm to his
heated brain, while the light of the coming day had
begun to streak the eastern heavens above the high
mountain peaks of the majestic Heidelberg in Baden.

Henceforth he was a wanderer upon the face of
earth. He made his way out of the city under cover
of darkness lest some might recognize him, and in
due time he arrived at the seaport where he shipped
aboard a merchant vessel. The next ten years he
spent upon the water and traversed nearly every
sea. In 1845 he landed at Vera Cruz and proceeded
to Mexico city, and was there when Gen. Scott on
September 14th, 1847, triumphantly entered that
city. The next season gold was discovered in
California and thither he wended his way. He
remained in the mountain gulches until 1860, and
then started on a trip across the continent, landing
at his former home in Charleston in the fall. The next
year when the war broke out, not wishing to take
sides with either faction, he set his face to the north
and in due time arrived at Quebec, Canada. Soon
after reaching that city he engaged to do light work
for an old professor who had retired from active life.
Being very fond of reading, the old gentleman gave
him free access to his library, where he passed his
leisure time.

One evening in overhauling the books he came
across an old parchment map, giving a rude outline

of Wisconsin and lake Michigan, with the course of three rivers traced across the territory running in a southwesterly direction, one of them being near the western shore of the lake. From near the lake's center, north and south, was a line drawn inland, terminating with a cross. The map was dated 1676, and marginal notes explained that the cross was located on a high eminence. This map interested him so greatly that he copied it, and soon after set out to visit and investigate the place described.

The advent of the hermit at the hill, of which mention has already been made, tallies with this date, or nearly so from the best evidence at hand. His coming was very mysterious, as was also his departure. No one has any knowledge of the exact date when he left, nor can anyone tell where he went after leaving the hill. It has been claimed by some that he was seen years afterwards in St. Louis, but as to this, there is nothing authentic. We submit here the writer's version of the "last interview," from the "Hermit of Holy Hill."

THE LAST INTERVIEW.

One summer evening late in June,
  Old Roman left his cottage sill,
To pray, and with the saints commune
  Upon the high and holy Hill.
As wandering on with book in hand,
  Now lost in solemn reverie,
He paused at intervals to stand,
  And tell his beads of rosary.

His pathway through the forest led,
  As up the steep ascent he strode;
The rising moon its luster shed,
  And lit the lonely pilgrim's road.
Anon the outer hill was passed,
  Thence downward through the deep defile,
He reached the Hermit's hut at last
  And halts before the rustic pile.

No cheerful ray of light awoke
　　To life that wretched human lair;
No sound the solemn stillness broke,
　　Save Roman's low and muttered prayer.
He prayed awhile and said his beads,
　　Then moved with slow and solemn pace,
To where the lonely pathway leads
　　Far upward to the shriving place.

Not far his footsteps had advanced,
　　When lo! he saw upon the left—
To where his eager vision glanced,
　　A form that seemed of life bereft!
Quick passing to the dreamer's side,
　　As moonbeams through the darkness broke,
He thought the Hermit he espied;
　　Then bending low old Roman spoke—

"Francois, is this thy form I see
　　Alone, with darkness overhead,
Out stretched beneath this ancient tree,
　　Say, is it thou, or art thou dead?
St. Mary! save my withered frame,
　　Old age hath made my vision weak—
I charge thee here, in heaven's name,
　　If thou art Francois, speak, O speak!"

He paused and waited for reply
　　An instant, while dead silence reigned—
He listened—First a long drawn sigh,
　　Then Francois answered, and explained—

"Yes, Roman, it is I, and thou
　　Hast chanced this meeting opportune;
The time has come, and, Roman now,
　　If thou canst bide yon passing moon,

Shall hear from me the Hermit's tale—
　　The secrets of my advent here,
And why I've trod this dismal vale
　　Through many a long and weary year."
Then Roman spoke—"Most gracious sire,
　　Though age forbids my lengthy stay
To hear thy tale, my strong desire
　　Doth all infirmities outweigh."

"Speak on, each circumstance relate,
　　To hear thee tell I here will stay
In spite of age or crippled state,
　　Though it outlasts the coming day"
"Then Roman, first thy form dispose
　　Recumbent by the side of mine;
Old age, like ours, demands repose
　　We both have lived man's lotted time.

"For I have seventy summers seen,
　　As from my record it appears,
And by thy aspect and thy mien
　　Thou art my senior still, in years."
So rested they, this aged twain,
　　That summer evening in the vale
Just as the moon began to wane.
　　The Hermit, then took up the tale.

TRADITIONAL HISTORY.

THERE is a number of circumstances connected with the traditional history of Holy Hill which tend to show that the place was visited by white men over two hundred years ago. It is quite certain, as authentic history relates, that the French missionaries coasted the western shore of Lake Michigan from the mouth of the Chicago river to Green Bay on several occasions during the summers from 1673 to 1679. The early adventurers had two objects in view; one, to explore the country west of Lake Michigan, also the Mississippi river and its tributaries between it and the lake; and the other object was the conversion of the Indian tribes to the Catholic religion. During these journeys up and down the lake, using only frail canoes, they were obliged to keep close to the shore. The nights were spent on the land, and they would frequently remain in one place for several days at a time. On such occasions it was their custom to erect crosses on some of the more prominent elevations.

Foremost among these early missionaries and

intrepid explorers was Father James Marquette. He,
in company with Louis Joliet, left Green Bay in
June 1673, and ascended the Fox river as far as
Portage, where they crossed to the Wisconsin, and
thence down that river to the Mississippi. They returned by ascending the Illinois and found their way
to Lake Michigan by that and the Chicago river,
landing where Chicago now stands in the early part
of September the same year. Marquette then proceeded to Green Bay by coasting along the west
shore of Lake Michigan, and arrived at his destination early in October. Again in October, 1674,
Father Marquette left the "portage" opposite
Sturgeon Bay, and coasted back to the mouth of the
Chicago river which he reached late in November.
On this trip he was accompanied by Pere and
Jacques Marquette, and ten canoes of Indians. They
were forty days making the journey, and as the
distance is less than two hundred miles they undoubtedly spent much of their time on shore. At
one time they were delayed five days, about fifteen
miles north of Milwaukee, in what is now the town
of Mequon. From subsequent evidence, it is believed
that at this time some of their party made a detour
inland, to the west, in hopes of finding Rock river
which they knew was not far away. The traditions
of the Indians say that they only went as far as
Holy Hill, and, failing to discover the river, they
erected a cross on the hill and returned to their
companions the next day. This theory is not im-
probable, and the journey might have been made, as
the distance to be traveled was less than twenty
miles inland.

The theory of this visit to the hill by white men at so early a date coincides with the description found on the hermit's map. Not only was the course of the journey traced out, but the cross designated the end of the journey. In addition to this particular cross there were several others located at different points along the lake shore from the mouth of the Chicago river to Green Bay. However, as the story of the hermit and his chart, is somewhat vague and uncertain, and like the history of his life, shrouded in mystery, such evidence must be regarded as unauthentic and uncertain.

Other adventurers followed the example set by Father Marquette, and for several years after, expeditions coasted the west shore of Lake Michigan between Chicago and Green Bay. Some of these, like Father Marquette, were endeavoring to establish missions to proselyte the different tribes of Indians, along the coast of the lake, to the Catholic faith. Other expeditions were made in the interest of trade or discovery. In October 1679, Louis Joliet and Sieur La Salle, in company with a number of others, made a similar coasting trip between the two places in the interest of the fur trade. They were nearly two months making the journey, and several 'times, owing to fierce storms, they were obliged to put to shore for safety.

Every Indian tribe, whose haunts were in the vicinity of Holy Hill, had a tradition, and firmly believed, that white men visited the hill very many years ago. In June 1844, Charles Frederick Hecker settled on land on the east shore of Pike Lake. At that time there was a large family of Pottawatomies

encamped near where he built his house. Old Kewaskum was their chief and they remained there a
number of years after the white settlers came. Mr.
Hecker, who was an old bachelor and lived alone,
was a very eccentric man, but was on very
friendly terms with the Indians, especially old Kewaskum. He used to relate how, after the work
was done, he and the old chief would sit on a log
and smoke for hours together. One evening as they
sat facing Pulford's hill, a short distance to the east,
their conversation turned to the object before them.
Suddenly old Kewaskum, pointing to the south, said
—"About an hour's walk in that direction is a hill
larger than this. I have heard my father tell that
white men came there many years ago and placed a
cross on the top of it. I can't tell how many years
ago it was, but my father said that his grand-father
was there at the time it was done."

Other tribes in the same locality had the same
tradition. Away back in the early "forties," when
the first settlers came in, there were several families
of the Menomonies scattered along the Oconomowoc
river from below Loew's lake on the south, to
Fries' lake on the east. Old Monches was the chief
of this tribe at the time, and was always on friendly
terms with the white people. Living in the vicinity
of the hill, whenever by chance it was alluded to, he
would become greatly interested and loved to tell of
how his tribe was knowing to the fact that white
men once came from Lake Michigan many years
before and planted a cross on its top. When speaking of the event he would always illustrate his story
by marking the shape of a cross, either in the snow,

sand or whatever soft substance happened to be the most conveniently at hand. Though he could not explain just the number of years that had passed since then, yet he was positive that it happened, and many, many years ago.

It may seem strange to say, as it is sad to admit, that the remains of both Kewaskum and Monches, after their death, were subjected to most shameful and ghoulish usage, and at the hands of a race for which they had shown great friendship, while living. Both shared a similar fate, for each, after he had been buried over twenty years, was dug up from his humble, shallow grave by relic hunters and his bones left to bleach upon the surface or to be scattered by the winds of earth.

Old Kewaskum died near Mud lake in the town Shields, Dodge county, about the year of 1857, and was buried on Indian (now Barber's) island, on Rock River, about four miles north of Hustisford. His body was dug up by a doctor and some others in the summer of 1878, and his beads, ornaments and other relics worn by him at burial are now in the hands of a party in Hartford. Old Monches died about the year of 1848, while living by the Oconomowoc river near the residence of the late John Whelan of Erin. Nearly thirty years later some curiosity seekers found his grave, and some others of his tribe, on a little knoll about a half mile east from the village that bears his name. They unearthed his remains and those of others and left their bones uncovered, where they lay until a hand more humanely disposed reinterred them. But while the graves of these noble chiefs were desecrated, yet their names were made lasting; for each has a place in Washington County named after him; Kewaskum near the north, and Monches on the south, county line.

From the foregoing it is seen that there is a number of circumstances connected with Holy Hill, which argues a strong probability of its having been visited by the French missionaries as early as, or previous to, 1679. But in the absence of authentic proof, it may not be admitted as a historical fact. Be that as it may, the place has since gained a history and a notoriety that time will never obliterate. Those who visit the place, although they may not be christians, are deeply impressed with its beauties, natural and artificial. To the christian, devout and sincere, there are but few places that will call from them greater homage or more adoration than Holy Hill. As evidence of the gratitude for blessings received, by devout christians, the following "thank offering," by one who received favors at the hill, is submitted:

ORA PRO NOBIS.

Hail Mary! Queen of Earth and Heaven,
Thou priceless boon to mortals given!
To this, Thy favored Holy shrine,
Thy children come from every clime.
"Health of the sick," to Thee we fly,
In mercy listen to our cry:
"Hail, full of grace! Blessed art Thou"
Low at Thy feet we humbly bow.
Ora Pro Nobis.

O Mary, "Help of Christians," see
The suffering ones who come to Thee.
Along the narrow, winding way
Each weary pilgrim halts to pray.
Listen! The prayer ascends e'en now,
"Hail, Mary! blest indeed art Thou,"
Was ever music half so sweet—
The echoing prayer of this retreat?

Ora Pro Nobis.

"Mother of Christ"—"Mother most pure,"
Thy promises are always sure.
"Virgin most prudent—most renowned,"
With honor by our Saviour crowned.
"Hail, Mary, Hail, blessed art thou"
Before Thee men and angels bow,
While through the earth resounds the prayer.
Sweet mother grant Thy gracious care.

Ora Pro Nobis.

Thou art above all others blest;—
For see, on all Thy altars rest
Earth's fairest flowers—Emblems of love.
Sancta Maria, from above
On all who seek this Holy place
Bestow a gift of Heavenly grace.
Protect and comfort every child
Who prays, "Hail Mary undefiled!

Ora Pro Nobis."

MATTIE FRENCH CRESSEY.

PRE-HISTORIC.

Wisconsin, perhaps more than any other state in the Union, furnishes positive proof of the existence of a race of people who once inhabited this continent, but which have long since become extinct and are absolutely lost to history; a race which, from all the evidence we can command, did not differ essentially in form, size and proclivity from our own; certainly, not more than do we from the aborigines that have been driven from the domain which we now possess.

Positive evidence of this lost tribe, or "pre-historic men," as some writers term them, is found in the tumuli or earth-mounds which they built and which proved to be more lasting than they. These structures which they erected and left to time and our wonder and contemplation, are found distributed over the greater part of the state. In nearly every instance we find that their locations were advantageously chosen with reference to ease of transportation, observation and defense. Generally they are found upon the high and steep banks of the larger rivers and lakes.

Some of the mounds appear to have been built as receptacles for the dead, while others are supposed to have been altars of worship. Some are built in the form of beasts, birds and reptiles, and even some are in profile of a man or a woman. Many of these earthworks resemble fortifications and to all appearances were used as places of refuge and defense from other tribes. In the construction of many there is seen a marked regularity in form, plan and detail, showing a commendable degree of engineering skill on the part of the builders, and which compares favorably with the accepted ideas of modern fortification.

For the reason that it must have taken a race of people, possessed of ordinary genius, to construct such huge and lasting monuments as are found, and for the further reason that it required a vast amount of labor, is precluded the faintest surmise that they were ever built by the Indian tribes; but rather is shown that they must have been the work of a more enlightened and energetic race. No Indian was ever known to have any conception of building, further than to construct a rude and temporary wigwam, and as to labor, he abhorred that above all things else.

Not alone these mounds, we find other evidence of the existence of this ancient race, showing very conclusively that they lived in an age more remote, and that they were possessed of a degree of civilization far in advance of their dusky and indolent followers. This evidence is seen in the many articles of domestic use that are found scattered over the surface of the ground in many localities throughout the state; particularly those utensils which are made from stone and copper. These relics of the lost race include a variety of implements such as axes, knives, drills, needles, spades, mauls, chisels, lances, spear points, arrow heads and many more. Those fashioned from copper are often finely wrought and some are hardened by pressure, the only method yet known to us for hardening that peculiar metal.

At various times specimens of these implements have been submitted to the Indians for examination, and they were questioned as to whether they had any knowledge or tradition of their origin. In every instance they have been free to admit that they knew nothing as to the cause of their presence here, nor anything of those who made them. For the reason that the prior race of men built so many wonderful and lasting mounds, the learned arch-aeologists have given them the name of "mound builders," but by what name they were known at the date of their existence the most profound anti-quarian has failed to discover.

There were many traces of the mound builders still extant in Washington county when the early settlers first came in, though these have since been nearly all obliterated, either by cultivation, or the persistent delving of the curiosity and relic seeker. There is no evidence that this early race ever dwelt in the vicinity of Holy Hill, for not a single mound, after their style, was ever discovered in the town of Erin. Though their homes might not have been there, still there is plenty of evidence that this was either their favorite hunting ground or a territory much coveted, and perhaps the scene of many contests. This conclusion is reached from the fact that there have been more stone and copper implements found, within a radius of five miles from Holy Hill, than within any other equal area of ground in the state. The writer has alone, within the past twenty years, secured over fifty fine copper specimens that were picked up near the hill, in addition to which, other relic hunters, notably, F. S. Perkins of Burlington, Wis., and W. C. Wyman of Chicago, Ill. have carried away a large number which they purchased from farmers residing near the hill.

The nearest mounds to Holy Hill, yet discovered, were on the north shore of Pike Lake, just five miles, nearly due north. These were very prominent when the country was first settled, but they are all now so completely leveled that none, excepting the very earliest settlers, could point out the place where they once stood. They were located on the south point of the north shore of the lake, just back of where the ice houses now stand, and where the bank rises abruptly from the water's edge to a height of forty feet. They were built like a fortification, enclosing about an acre of land. These ancient earthworks were in a good state of preservation as late as 1856, and in that year the writer made a survey of them. The accompanying plat, which is eighty feet to the inch, is a fair representation as they then existed. The large mound in the extreme southeast corner, was then fifteen feet high and sixty feet in diameter at the base. From its commanding position, standing on the top, every point of the lake could be readily seen. To the west were two smaller ones, the last being turtle shaped with head to the lake. From the tip of the turtle's tail a well defined

wall of earth extended east to the steep bank of the
lake's shore completing the enclosure.

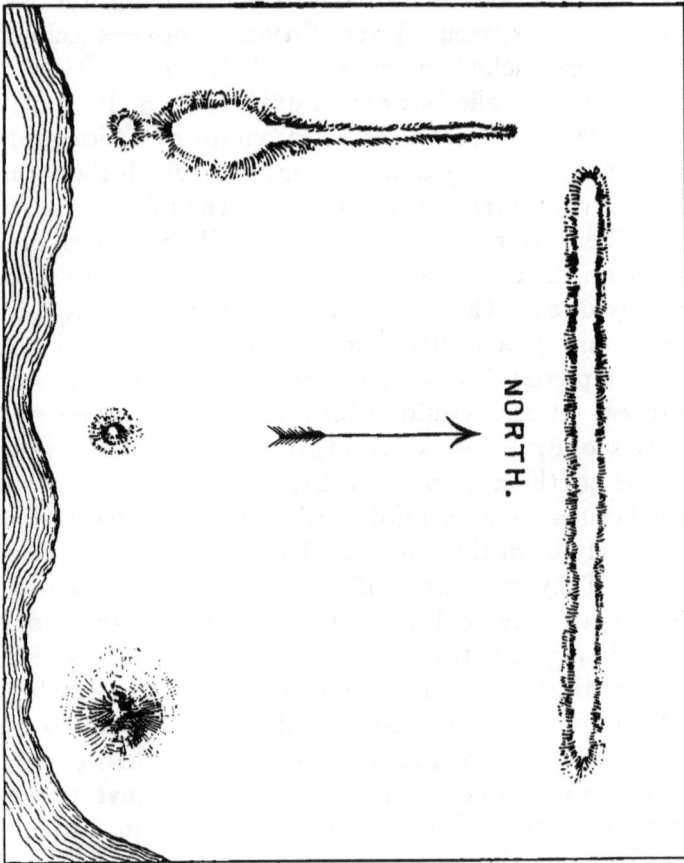

A number of other mounds were found in Washington county by the early settlers, principally on
the Milwaukee river in the towns of Trenton, Bar-
ton and Kewaskum. Though there are many beau-

tiful lakes in the vicinity of Holy Hill, as Fries' lake, two miles east, Loew's lake, two miles south and McConville's and Murphy's lakes two miles southwest, yet around the margin of either of these lakes, no trace of any works of the mound builders was ever discovered.

On the banks of Rock River, some fifteen miles to the west, these mounds are numerous and of prodigious size. Just east from Hustisford, where a small stream empties into the "rapids" of that river, is a steep bank rising to the height of over a hundred feet. On this high bluff are thirteen large mounds standing in a direct line north and south. In the fall of 1867, while returning from a days hunting, the writer chanced to pass by this long row of mounds. Evidently some one had just been searching in one of them, for the earth removed was fresh. They had cut a trench from the outside which penetrated to the center and base. Near the pile of earth which had been thrown out lay seventeen skulls. The sun was sinking in the west and, when twilight ushered in the night, we were left in darkness and alone, to contemplate on the surrounding dead of ages past. It was fitting time for solemn reverie and musing, and we called the place *Butte des Morts*—The hill of the dead.

BUTTE DES MORTS.

As the fast setting sun its last rays is shedding
  O'er a landscape to beauty and grandeur allied,
Alone by the mounds of the ancients I'm treading,
  And wonder what years have elapsed since they died.

Before me Rock river runs rapid, and leaping
  Over rocks that for ages obstructed its flow,
And I feel that the tribe, who around me is sleeping,
  Oft gazed on this scene in the dim long ago.

Perhaps on this high elevation of grandeur,
  On the orient bank of this beautiful stream,
As sentries they stood, while guarding from danger
  Their tribe against foes that were lurking unseen.

And oft on this hill, by rude breast works protected,
  Like heroes have fought to the last for their home;
'Mid death and disaster, yet cool and collected,
  Struck home the death blows with their weapons of stone!

Perhaps some dark youth, fired by love and devotion,
　Enticed his rude maiden apart from the tribe,
To the spot where I'm standing, and told with emotion
　His tale of true love, as she clung to his side.

How they lived or they loved, how came or departed,
　Is only conjecture to us that are now;
If hero or coward, if true or false-hearted—
　We know they existed but cannot tell how.

For the long flight of years, by ages, we number,
　Since they roamed o'er these hills and valleys between;
Erected these mounds, where they silently slumber,
　Yet left us no records when quitting the scene.

In vain may we delve in these mounds and uncover
　Their mould'ring forms—All our efforts are vain,
For science and research shall fail to discover
　Their origin—When they departed or came.

Sleep on then, lost tribe, for a mightier nation
　Than yours has since met with a similar fate;
Like you, have been swept from the face of creation,
　By us who must follow them, sooner or late.

How vain then, proud man, all thy boast and ambition,
　How frail are the structures you're building to stay!
Convulsions of nature may hurl to perdition
　Your works, ere the sun has awakened the day.

Then sleep in contentment, securely forever,
　No mortal that's living your mission shall guess:
Here safe be thy rest, on the banks of Rock river,
　No spot in creation more lovely than this.

But the shadows of night are falling around me,
  Obscuring my vision, all nature is still;
And fain would I leave, but the spell that has bound me
  Compels me to linger awhile on the hill.

The sun has withdrawn, but the moon is now shining,
  'Tis painting this picture with splendor anew;
Each star pays its tribute, together combining,
  Hath rendered each object distinct to my view.

Now I list to sound of the murm'ring river
  As it flows o'er the rocks and never is still,
While above and beyond and blending together,
  I hear the low hum of the wheel in the mill.

Mid this scene and the music of waters I leave you,
  With a sense of true beauty, you chose your last bed,
Though men who now live, of the mounds may relieve you,
  And level the tombs on the hills of the dead.

When the trumpet is sounded by angels, compelling
  Us all to come forth, and when time is no more,
You'll rise from the depths of your last earthly dwelling
  And stand with the rest on the grand *Butte des Morts.*